M . .

NEGOTIATION TRAINING
THROUGH GAMING

NEGOTIATION TRAINING THROUGH GAMING

Strategies, Tactics and Manoeuvres

Elizabeth M Christopher

Larry E Smith

Kogan Page, London
Nichols/GP Publishing, New York

This book is dedicated to the memory of Erica Bates and Barry Moore

First published in 1991

Kogan Page Limited
120 Pentonville Road
London N1 9JN

© Christopher and Smith, 1991

British Library Cataloguing in Publication Data

A CIP record for this book is available from the British Library.

ISBN 0 7494 0370 5

First published in the USA in 1991
by Nichols/GP Publishing
11 Harts Lane, East Brunswick
NJ 08816 USA

Library of Congress Cataloging-in-Publication Data

Christopher, Elizabeth M.
    Negotiation training through gaming: strategies, tactics, and manoeuvres/Elizabeth Christopher and Larry Smith.
        p.   cm.
    Includes bibliographical references and index.
    ISBN 0-89397-408-0: $39.95
    1. Negotiation in business-Simulation methods.
    2. Management games.   I. Smith, Larry E.   II. Title.
    HD58.6.C47   1991
    658.4-dc20

Typeset by DP Photosetting, Aylesbury, Bucks
Printed and bound in Great Britain by
Clays Ltd, St Ives plc

Contents

Acknowledgements

We would like to acknowledge our debt to the following people for their assistance in various ways with the writing of this book:

- Professor Denis Breen, Dean of the School of Business and Public Administration, Charles Sturt University, Bathurst, New South Wales, who gave Elizabeth leave to travel to and fro between Australia and Hawaii to complete the book.
- Vincent Ferravanti, Director of Systems Analysis, AUGAT Manufacturing Company, Mansfield, Massachusetts, for his permission to include THE MRP GAME.
- Joyce Gruhn, Institute of Culture and Communication, East-West Center, for her unfailing support on the computer.
- The late Michael Harvey, formerly lecturer in industrial relations, School of Business, Charles Sturt University, Bathurst, New South Wales for giving us access to all his notes.
- The late Dr Barry Moore, former management consultant of Sydney, for permission to include material for BLUEPRINT.
- Participants in the certificate course in training management at the Australian Institute of Management Training College, Sydney, who played and critiqued many of the games in this book.
- Janice Rafferty, School of Business, Charles Sturt University, Mitchell, for listening so patiently to progress reports.
- John Sleigh, for permission to borrow from his book *Making Learning Fun*.
- Students of the Japan-American Institute of Management Science, Hawaii, who field-tested many of the games and simulations, and provided constructive and encouraging feedback.
- Otto van Veen, Management Development Centre, Mijgnrode, Breukglen, Netherlands, for permission to include OTTO'S GAME.

Part I
Background and Technique

Introduction
Negotiation Training through Games and Simulations: How it Works

Almost everything in life is negotiable: goods, services, information, technology, income, position, status, reputation and public image. All human activity provides a setting for this delicate and complex process. The personalities of the negotiators are crucial – but the process must be de-personalized if it is to be successful.

Negotiation is most commonly defined as an activity between two or more people who want or need something from each other. For example Fisher and Ury (1988:vi) take negotiation to mean the ways in which people deal with their differences by trying to 'get to yes without going to war'. Wall (1985:4) defines negotiation as the process by which the relevant parties coordinate an exchange of goods or services – as opposed to bargaining, which he suggests is more manipulative, and debate, which he takes to be specific behaviour within the overall process of negotiation.

These definitions conceptualize negotiation as something essentially pragmatic, practical and emotionally neutral. However, there is another way of looking at it. Negotiation may be seen as the means by which we cope with and allocate priorities between basically conflicting interests. Others take this argument even further: they see negotiation as the use of information and power to affect the behaviour of others.

Some negotiations are virtually never-ending, as in industrial relations; some are momentary, as when two people argue who will go first through the door. But all are characterized by the same kind of process, by which the negotiators attempt to move each other towards cooperation and concession. It is a process that people try to accomplish by fair means or foul: most people, at times, are tempted to resort to hostile, destructive behaviour such as aggression or coercion, manipulation or stubbornness. The frequency and style with which they resort to these will depend on a combination of circumstances and individual personality. Usually people learn to adopt more friendly and constructive behaviour if their negotiations are to be successful – particularly if a relationship needs to be created and maintained over time.

Thirty years ago there was no substantial body of literature on negotiation as a social process; today the topic is a cross-disciplinary study including organizational behaviour, psychology, sociology, economics – and gaming. We believe simulation games are the ideal media for training students in negotiation techniques because they are themselves a form of negotiation. People gather together in a structured setting in which they negotiate a number of roles and rules to achieve some kind of predetermined objective. Then they look back on the whole process and ask themselves and each other what happened, to whom and why, and with what result.

This book is about the use of simulations and games to improve the skills needed for successful negotiation. It is written for all teachers of negotiating practices – in the training departments of large and small organizations, in schools, colleges and universities. The book describes a number of games and is designed to identify negotiation strategies – the broad plans that negotiators devise to achieve a predetermined goal; tactics – the components of those plans; and manoeuvres – the behaviour they use to improve their position for attack or defence (Wall 1985). Guidelines are given on how to design or adapt any game structure to suit the particular purposes of a game director. All the games have been used effectively to train undergraduate business students, MBA and other graduate students, managers and educators in America, Australia, Britain, Europe, Japan and Papua New Guinea.

The book was written in the knowledge that there is already a substantial literature on the use of simulation games to study negotiation skills, that considerable research has been carried out on the subject and that some criticisms have been made of their value as teaching tools. For example, Donahue et al (1984) note three specific ways in which real-life negotiations are likely to differ from simulations:

1. Aggressive or attacking tactics are usually employed less frequently in simulated negotiations than in real life, because participants in a simulation are not so much affected person-

ally by the outcome as in real life and are not accountable for it to the same extent as are 'real' negotiators.

2. For similar reasons, players of simulation games are more likely to use integrating and responding tactics than are their real-life counterparts. For example in most industrial disputes the union representatives are likely to make the most demands, while management tends to adopt a more defensive position; in a similar but simulated situation the bargainers are usually more flexible with respect to each other's goals.

3. Most labour-management negotiations are restricted by rather rigid conventions about who presents proposals, how they are evaluated, and so on. In a simulated negotiation the players are likely to feel freer to experiment with less conventional behaviour.

These observations are well founded: authentic negotiations – especially if recorded on audio or videotape – provide much better material for the study of negotiation than do simulated ones. However, the book breaks new ground in emphasizing how most effectively to use simulations as training tools to sharpen partici-pants' negotiation skills rather than for the study of negotiation per se.

Simulations can persuade participants to experiment with new approaches to negotiation in a context where their effectiveness can be evaluated without risk of disastrous consequences. Moreover, success in simulation can encourage players later to attempt more 'I win–you win' tactics in real-life bargaining and less 'I win–you lose'.

Historically, in westernized countries there has been an indus-trial divide between management and labour and the term 'industrial relations' has been tacitly accepted to describe battle conditions between unions and employers. In this context the activity of 'human resources management' becomes ideologically and politically suspect – tarred with the colour of worker-exploitation. Nowadays, however, there is urgent need for both developing and developed countries to find new markets in an increasingly competitive and globalized marketplace. Therefore all aspects of management, including personnel management, are becoming recognized as 'industrial relations'. It is in this changing climate of industrial democracy that the essentially democratic process of gaming simulation has its greatest value.

The book is divided into five chapters. Chapter 1 describes the actual process of designing or adapting a simulation game to fit the purposes of the client. Chapter 2 offers a number of examples of what we call 'focus games' – short activities designed to draw participants' attention to key negotiation issues and stimulate them to take an active interest in exploring these issues. Chapter 3 is about roleplays and improvisations, while Chapter 4 describes a number of simulations.

Thus the book contains examples of the whole range of negotiation games, from simple classroom exercises that offer a few moments of thought-provoking activity, through team games and syndicate work, to quite long and complex simulations. All have been chosen to isolate and identify different kinds of negotiating behaviour – argued in the literature to contribute directly to expertise in negotiation, specifically for the achievement of organizational goals. They are all discussed from the viewpoint of the game director – the arch-negotiator between the material to be learned and the people who need to learn it. There is an alphabetical list by topic of all the games in the book, and they are also listed alphabetically by name and annotated. An example is included of an evaluation questionnaire, and there is an annotated bibliography.

We hope that you will find *Negotiation Training through Gaming* entertaining as well as instructive. Whether you have decades of experience in directing games or virtually none at all, we are confident you will be a better negotiator when you have worked through these activities. We wish you every success.

Chapter 1
The Do's and Don'ts of Designing, Adapting, Directing and Debriefing

An overview of the problems

Training films often show what not to do before demonstrating more effective methods. We want to use the same technique by describing what to avoid in the process of designing or adapting a simulation game. Our example is the following cautionary tale.

Sally is a staff-development officer who wanted to use a simulation as a diagnostic exercise for the managers of her small manufacturing organization, which was having problems marketing an expanded range of products under a recently introduced organizational-development scheme. Sally didn't know of an existing game to meet her needs so she read a book on how to design simulation games and started working out a scenario.

Her first problem was where to begin the story – two years ago? Next week? The year 2000? The book didn't have any information on this so Sally assumed the matter wasn't important and the scenario might as well start 'next week'. She arranged for the action to begin with a flood of orders hitting the factory, resulting in disarray at the loading dock. Then – leaving tedious details to the imagination of the players – she moved on to describe six or seven role outlines including the respective supervisors of quality control, dock loading and distribution. She added some ground rules for their behaviour and an evaluation form which neutral observers would complete after the game. Lastly she gave the simulation a title: BOTTLENECK. Having now completed what the book described as the essentials of the exercise – scenario, roles, rules and a monitoring device for evaluating the progress of the simulation – she handed the whole manuscript to her typist, Jane, with instructions about preparing rolecards and other organizational details.

As it happened, Jane's greatest wish was to be an actress; she attended drama classes three nights a week and thought it a fantastic idea to use a roleplaying game as a training exercise. She described the simulation in detail to anybody interested enough to listen – and plenty of people were. The next day a stunned Sally had an angry dock-loading supervisor storming into her office demanding to know why Sally had accused her behind her back of causing production bottlenecks.

Then the cost accountant came to complain he'd been left out of the list of characters and wasn't even consulted about the details Sally had thought too trivial to mention. He added this was typical of her usual high-handed attitude and it was about time she stopped behaving as if she were the only person in the firm with ideas to contribute. Then the union representative expressed his disapproval of what he considered to be time-and-motion studies being conducted under the cover of training sessions. At this point Sally's chief executive officer, newly appointed and anxious not to make waves, told her to drop the whole idea. Later, when somebody in the staff canteen quite innocently mentioned simulation games, Sally burst into tears.

Sally's problem was not with games as such, nor with the way she went through the drill. That was correct as far as it went. But prescriptive rules for game design – or for adapting existing games – may overlook the need to assess the unique characteristics of the relevant organisation before trying to represent it in game form.

Moreover, Sally neglected to take account of several other essential variables. Below is a list of the external and internal factors all games directors need to consider.

The external factors of simulation game design
The brief
What exactly are you being asked to achieve? What is the *real*

problem your training programme is supposed to solve? First explore the needs of your client (your employer, your manager, the person to whom you are accountable). What are their expectations of your activity? The provision of training is a cost, like wages, and has to be accounted for, so your employers expect you to earn your keep and justify their releasing people out of the workforce to participate in your simulation. This is another reason why monitoring is essential to any simulation game: it should confirm that issues critical to players' real-life needs were raised and dealt with in the course of the game.

You need the sanction, approval and support of those concerned before you embark on the project – particularly when managing directors or chief executive officers (CEOs) are new and unsure of themselves. This may call for some sales skill on your part: some employers still believe workers are not paid to play games in company time. Be well prepared with a rational defence of your proposal that includes time/cost factors, the kind of learning the participants are likely to derive, and the benefits likely to accrue to the company both in the short and long term. Compare these estimates (favourably – otherwise you're in trouble!) with those for another kind of training programme, like a lecture or demonstration; describe how the simulation will be evaluated; and support your arguments with evidence, by recalling the success of similar programmes in the past in this organization and/or elsewhere.

The culture of the client organization

What are the purpose and product of the organization? What kinds of materials, people, technology does it employ? What kind of hierarchy does it have? Where does it get its supplies and information? You need to know the answers to at least some of these questions before you start directing gaming simulations with the organization's employees. The information will assist you in designing or adapting an appropriate simulation – or, just as importantly, in avoiding some designs. For example, if the group consists of specialists (in medicine, real estate, accountancy, law, etc) you may not find it helpful to create a realistic game setting for their respective fields. If you try to make a simulation too 'real', the participants may feel they know more about it than you do and may waste everybody's time disputing points of accuracy.

Try instead to discover *the spirit of the culture* of your client organization, and represent that culture somehow in your game. Just as people have their preferred problem-solving styles, so do organizations. We all know the phrase 'organizational behaviour' but we may sometimes forget that no two organizations behave exactly the same in their efforts to increase productivity and capture larger market shares. Some are on the cutting edge of innovation, others identify and specialize in a particular market niche. Others again are slow to change because of large capital investment in plant and machinery. In any case, the management and staff of competitive private companies operate on different assumptions from those of helping agencies, religious bodies or government departments. These critical differences in organization culture must be identified in simulation exercises and their implications explored for purposes of strategic game planning.

In the cautionary tale above, Sally's organization manufactured connectors for a number of regular client companies. Quality control and regular output were its most important considerations, but supervisors and staff had become conservative and complacent with security. Therefore, when senior management, looking to the long term, tried to introduce new technology and expand their product range, they were met with suspicion and even hostility in this small, democratic company whose members felt personally concerned with its success. Since it had a highly effective grapevine, spreading communication and providing immediate feedback to practically everything that happened in the organization, Sally probably would have done well to adopt the following strategy:

- tap into the grapevine to learn the nature of employees' fears about the proposed changes;
- identify key elements of company policy regarding the proposed changes;
- model both fears and proposals into the game scenario;
- design the whole project as a communication exercise and confidence-builder for the whole company;
- play it in collaboration with the personnel office and build the character of the union representative into the game.

In summary, when you take a brief to design a game, remember that the 'personality' of the organization will inevitably affect not only the process of the design but also the design itself. Therefore, when you've roughed out the outlines of your simulation, before finalizing it, discuss it with the client company and amend the format accordingly.

The personalities of the people involved in the exercise

A golden rule for any simulation of organizational change is that it should identify what elements of the game caused participants the most stress. This will give invaluable pointers to danger areas when the changes are actually implemented. However, to get this kind of sensitive feedback from players you have first to win their confidence that information derived from something so essentially trivial as a game can provide insights to the workplace.

In Sally's sad story, the dock-loading supervisor and the cost accountant were particularly alarmed at the prospect of a simulation game. This is not unusual. Many adults don't like the idea of making a game of their work; their problem-solving styles may need theoretical principles on which to create a plan of action before the action itself.

Alternatively, logistically-minded supervisors and accountants may well be inclined by temperament and professional training to work logically in linear progression through facts and figures in order to arrive at decisions based on empirical evidence. When such people enrol in management-training programmes they expect to be directed by specialists whose qualifications they recognize and respect. They expect to receive practical instruction they can relate directly to their work. They are likely to respond with suspicion, if not hostility, to the suggestion of a game as a problem-solving device. Others distrust games for different reasons: they intuitively feel the need to observe and reflect before being thrust into action. They want to watch, not to play.

On the other hand you will remember that in Sally's case, Jane thought the idea of a game was great. She seems to own a feelings/experience-based problem-solving style. So do many actors, teachers, social workers and salespeople, for example. In fact, the sales staff in Sally's company were quite happy with the idea of a simulation game – they actually went to the CEO and requested it go ahead, though he wasn't prepared to listen. They were 'Let's give it a go' kind of people, willing to take on trust Sally's assertion that the game might suggest ways they could do their job more efficiently and profitably.

The moral of the story is that when playing games it is safe to assume that any given group of players will demonstrate between them at least four major problem-solving styles: theoretical, practical, reflective and experiential (Kolb et al 1986). And though some will take to simulations like ducks to water, others will be more like horses. You can lead them to the fountain of knowledge but no power of yours can make them drink unless they have first tested it.

You will cater to all four learning styles if you follow this sequence:

1. Give participants some information in advance about the organizational problems the game seeks to model (theoretical).
2. Talk briefly about the advantages of such modelling exercises based on your professional experience (practical).
3. Validate the importance of observer roles in simulation activities (reflective).
4. Direct the simulation (experiential).
5. Debrief players afterwards with reference to theoretical, practical, reflective and experiential outcomes.

Your own background and personality as teacher and game director

We have stressed that the ways in which simulation games are presented, directed and debriefed will critically affect the responses of the players, irrespective of the actual content of the exercises (Christopher and Smith 1990). Thus it follows that you are the most important variable in the learning conveyed by any structured experience such as a game, roleplay, improvisation or simulation. You are the negotiator between the content of the exercise and the personalities of the people who take part in it. Therefore, as indicated above, you need to know how to vary your tactics to suit the group. You should be able to create, sustain and control a supportive environment for people assembled – by choice or command – for the express purpose of learning something.

Moreover, whether you are professional or volunteer, teacher or trainer, seasoned hand or novice, you should be capable of dealing with learners' *feelings* constructively, sympathetically and relatively impersonally. The rationale of simulation games is that they evoke emotions in the players – anger, amusement, frustration, elation, disappointment, hope, failure, success – *in order that* their owners afterwards can be shown how to relate their feelings cognitively to real-life problems and situations.

The experience of playing a simulation game, by itself, is not likely to 'teach' players anything, except perhaps that they do or do not like playing simulation games. It is your business to help them apply what happened in the game to the theoretical material they need to learn. If you can't give them that framework they are likely to find the whole thing a waste of time – and blame you for it.

However, many groups suffer from initial inertia: people would rather sit and listen passively than take active part in their own learning. So you may have to get them going. Don't spend too long talking: get the game under way as soon as you've introduced and explained its purposes. Some groups try to delay the inevitable by asking lots of questions, but don't allow yourself to be seduced into debate instead of drama. Describe the scenario, give them or let them choose active or observer roles and move them along into the experience of the game. Be on hand to assist with any major problems but otherwise keep quiet and don't interfere. Take notes (mental and written) of any behaviour that strikes you as particularly relevant. Monitor the activity with assistance from the neutral observers (maybe you've given them a checklist of behaviour to watch out for). Video the activity if possible.

When it's all over, call a plenary session (or build this into the structure of the game; see examples in later chapters).

There should always be some mechanism by which players can be brought to reflect methodically on what happened from a background of pre-existing knowledge, professional expertise and life experience. This is where you need some kind of evaluation or assessment instrument. It may be some report players have to fill out during or after the game: tangible evidence of what happened, and food for thought.

Finally, we draw your attention to our own problem-solving style throughout this book. You will observe that all our advice is practical rather than theoretical, experiential rather than abstract. Though there are some excellent texts from the US and the UK that emphasize simulation gaming as a process of logic, very little has been written on the more holistic methods that seem to be used by many successful game designers, based on a combination of experience, observation, theory and practice. If you want to direct simulations you need to be aware of the nuances of your particular learning style – and be willing to vary it in accordance with the situation and characteristics of each group you lead. As a game director you are a group leader (Christopher and Smith 1987). Like all leadership behaviour, your verbal and non-verbal cues must be feelings-oriented to appeal to the experiential learners in your group but so well organized that the more practical people feel comfortable. You need to validate observer roles by using spectators' reports to help you generalize from players' experience of the game to real-world problems and situations.

If you don't feel comfortable with such a range of styles, then by all means give simulations a miss. It is no reflection on your teaching skills if you decide this is not for you: there are many other ways of encouraging students to take control of their own learning. You are the best judge of your own background and temperament and it is up to you to select the teaching tools that best serve your purpose.

Moreover, if we have failed to deter you so far, here are more words of warning. You will need to be as skilful in debriefing as in directing a simulation game. For example, if you try to generalize too widely on the basis of a single playing, you may receive protests that you are drawing unjustified conclusions from inadequate data. Players may resist (quite rightly) any attempts on your part to tell them what their behaviour 'means'. But though you need to avoid being judgmental you also need to focus attention on relevant issues or players' discussion is likely to go off at tangents. There are so many interesting ideas generated during a simulation game that players have a great variety of experiences they want to share. Thus, in debriefing, as during the game itself, you have to move as required up and down the whole range of leadership behaviour.

Feedback and evaluation

It is not only for the sake of the reflective learners in your group that it is a good plan to have neutral observers in a simulation as well as more formal evaluation techniques like questionnaires.

Every independent evaluation of players' behaviour is welcome in the assessment of a game's effectiveness. One of the biggest criticisms of simulation games is that participants frequently don't seem to learn very much from them, though poor debriefing and assessment methods may be the culprits, not the games. More often than not the game director is the only person who has seen the whole of the action as a non-participant observer. Inevitably, their biases will affect the way they debrief the players afterwards.

There are other methods of reducing this bias, apart from reports from independent observers. For example, players should always complete a feedback questionnaire after the exercise (see the sample in Appendix 2) and other measures include:

- follow-up reports, after at least several weeks, by their supervisors and managers on any work-related benefits players seem to have acquired from the simulation;
- reports by players to their supervisors on what they think they learned from the simulation and how they expect to apply this to their work;
- any other feedback from the workplace.

In summary, six external factors are critical variables in game design and selection:

- your brief: the objectives for the activity;
- the degree of support from the client organization for the project;
- the nature of the organizational culture from which the brief emerged and how this is represented in the simulation;
- the personalities and problem-solving (learning) styles of the players and how these affect their responses to the simulation;
- your own background and personality and how these affect your introduction of the simulation, your processing and discussion of it;
- evaluation of the exercise as a learning strategy.

The internal factors of game design

Now let's look more closely at four basic components of the game itself.

The represented setting

This should be a naturalistic scenario, but not necessarily realistic. In other words, the action of the game may be set in outer space or Timbuctoo or Tit-Willow Land, but within the setting, however fanciful, the actors will behave naturally, as themselves.

Roles: agendas for the key participants

A reason frequently given by students for their reluctance to role-play is that they find it impossible to 'act as if I were somebody I'm not'. This is a reasonable statement because nobody can behave other than as themselves and they should not be asked to try (Via and Smith 1979).

Rules: the ground rules players must observe

The only rule you need to give them is that they are constrained within a setting that represents a particular set of problems and therefore *are bound by behaviour relevant to that setting.*

Scoring and/or monitoring

There must be evaluation of players' performance during the game, related afterwards to real-life outcomes. Examples of monitoring devices are actual scores (for instance if the exercise is a competitive team game); checklists which players and/or neutral observers have to keep to mark the progress of the game; and videotaping.

Short simulations with fairly small groups are often very suitable for recording. The camera can be set up and left running and after a few moments most players seem to forget its presence. The tape can be stopped periodically and replayed during a break in the game so players can discuss what stage in the negotiation they appear to have reached and debate future strategy; or debriefing can be left till the end. On the other hand there may be observer roles built into the represented setting, such as 'a reporter from the local newspaper'. Also, observers may be non-players, privately briefed in advance or given written suggestions about the kind of behaviour they should be looking out for – or asked to record what they see without discrimination so you can select from these impressions afterwards.

However you organize it, this four-part, constantly interacting pattern of setting, roles, rules and observation will convert the process of any game into an open system: its activity will promote students' self-directed learning through continuous feedback to what actually happens in the 'real world' – as summarized by the following flowchart:

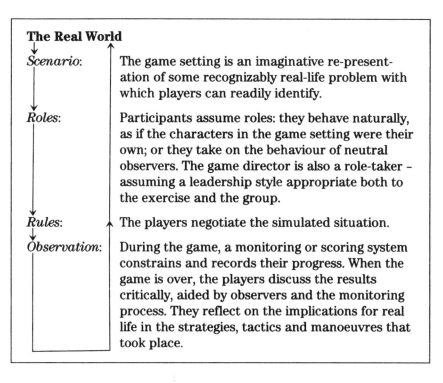

The Real World

Scenario:	The game setting is an imaginative re-present-ation of some recognizably real-life problem with which players can readily identify.
Roles:	Participants assume roles: they behave naturally, as if the characters in the game setting were their own; or they take on the behaviour of neutral observers. The game director is also a role-taker – assuming a leadership style appropriate both to the exercise and the group.
Rules:	The players negotiate the simulated situation.
Observation:	During the game, a monitoring or scoring system constrains and records their progress. When the game is over, the players discuss the results critically, aided by observers and the monitoring process. They reflect on the implications for real life in the strategies, tactics and manoeuvres that took place.

Special considerations: industrial relations and multiculturalism

We cannot finish this chapter without reference to two specific areas of negotiation training where games, roleplays, improvisations and simulations are particularly helpful but which also contain particular pitfalls for the unwary game director. These areas are industrial relations and cross-cultural training.

Industrial relations (IR)

This phrase refers to all negotiation between employers and

employees; that is, between management and labour or the representatives of labour unions. Particularly in the UK and Australia, the study of IR has reached mammoth proportions because of the relative strength of the trade unions and a historic tradition of confrontation – of management/worker bargaining, a spirit of 'them against us', rather than 'We're all in this together'.

IR simulations are particularly interesting to training officers, personnel managers and human-resource-development practitioners when they incorporate a classic three-phase format that not only models the actual process of IR negotiation as practised in the UK and Australia but also provides a design framework for many other negotiation games. In the introduction to this book we mentioned a general criticism of IR simulations: that they fail to elicit the kind of behaviour that management and labour representatives exhibit in real life. Nevertheless, IR simulations can do the following:

- coach participants in making preparations before bargaining opens;
- expose players to likely bargaining strategies;
- remind them of what needs to be done to ratify the bargain after striking it.

Thus there should be three phases in an IR simulation if it is to model real life.

1. Pre-negotiation, preparation phase
Players must be given the opportunity to predict the kind of concessions the opposition might be likely to offer, the counter-concessions that might be made; and their costs and benefits. An agenda for players in this pre-negotiation stage might include the following questions:

- What do we *really* want to get out of this? (Establishment of objectives.)
- What series of fallback positions can we prepare?
- Are our major arguments sound and reasonable?
- What counter-arguments should we be prepared for?
- Are their arguments likely to be weak or strong? Why?
- What is likely to be the final cost of these claims and counter-claims?

- What is the cost to us if we lose?
- What is the benefit to us if we win?

If participants in IR simulations are encouraged to consider options like these early in the preparation phase, they have the opportunity to modify their objectives and major arguments accordingly. Also, it is worth remembering that in real life IR negotiators are very much aware of certain factors that most IR simulations omit, such as existing agreements, relevant legislation, previous cases or precedents, policies and rules of the organization, customs and practices of the organization, comparative circumstances in other organizations and performance and profitability to ensure employment.

These are considerations you need in the game scenario. And when you write the roles you might want to include a few 'consultants' who take no active part in the game but serve as resource people and observers. These characters might include:

- supervisors;
- workgroup leaders;
- union members;
- managers;
- representatives from the department of industrial relations;

and so on. Give these characters a copy of the scenario, ask them to get together in this first phase of the game to improvise more detail for information to players on request.

2. The actual negotiation
Your game description should include:

- meeting time and place;
- a copy of previous minutes;
- agenda paper.

After the negotiation, these are the kind of questions to ask when debriefing the players (or you may wish to write them up as notes to participants prior to the simulation):

- Did participants make their respective positions clear?
- Did the disputants outline clearly and concisely the benefits of their respective proposals and expand on them as required?
- Did they really listen to and try to understand the opposition?
- Did they try to pick up hints of a possible compromise?
- Did everybody refrain from being antagonistic or insulting?
- Was everybody flexible? Did they keep an open mind?
- Were they reasonable, calm, prepared to compromise, and fair?
- Did they resist getting bogged down on particular issues early in the negotiation?
- Did anybody promise more than they could deliver?
- Did either party ask for an adjournment (for example to reconcile differences among themselves)?

3. The end of the negotiation

After the bargain is struck (or players have failed to strike one) participants need to be reminded in debriefing of the need in real life for:

- written confirmation of the details of what was agreed on, with copies for both sides;
- understanding of the implications about what might be discussed later;
- setting a date for implementation of the agreement;
- leaving the door open for future negotiations.

This last may not seem easy if the simulated negotiation has not proved very constructive, but it needs to be stressed. It is unrealistic in most cases to declare negotiation at an end because agreement has not been reached. Sooner or later some consensus will have to be found and now is as good a time as any.

International and cross-cultural games

Many of the games and simulations in this book were trialled with non-native English speakers, and with groups whose members came from different countries and cultures. We hope you also will have the opportunity to direct these games in international settings because you will undoubtedly find the experience interesting and rewarding on many levels. However, be warned that any feelings some participants might have about simulation games will be intensified in the presence of one or more of the variables below.

Language discrepancy

Some players may be native English speakers while others are not, and the native speakers may try to use their greater language fluency to negotiate more favourable conditions for themselves. Though the non-native speakers may become aware this is happening and resent it, they are often powerless to do anything about it without your help. You may in fact want this power imbalance to occur so you can discuss it later; or you may want to empower the weaker players with some strategy other than language – special knowledge, for example, or more material resources.

Taboos

Players may find some roles in a simulation to be undignified or insulting on racial, religious, cultural or national grounds. On one occasion we cast a Japanese professor as a streetmarket vendor, whereupon one of the observers, also Japanese, indicated plainly he thought we had insulted his distinguished fellow-national. If you want to play games in international settings you need to familiarize yourself with the social, class and religious taboos and norms of group members. A colleague of ours once caused a great argument when he asked a group of Malaysian Muslim students to draw their self-portraits, since to do so would offend their religion.

Local knowledge

Participants who are foreign to you may have to work in real life with constraints you know nothing about. They may become frustrated if you work from your agenda in ignorance of their needs. The first time we visited Papua New Guinea (PNG) we ran a workshop for educators, community workers and healthcare professionals on the use of simulations, games and roleplays to educate local women to negotiate the problem of domestic violence – otherwise known as wife-bashing. Because our audience was too polite to correct us, we took some time to recognize that much of our material was useless to this particular audience because it was based on the assumption that their clients would be literate. One of the games we eventually designed to surmount this problem is MERI WANTAIM MAN which is described in the next chapter.

Feedback

As indicated above, if your participants are markedly different from you by reason of race, nationality, colour, creed – even age or gender – they may be reluctant to interrupt you, much less correct you, when your material is irrelevant for their purposes. Such groups may be so quiet and attentive you can be misled into talking too much and listening too little: the whole programme may be of limited value to those who need it most. Constant feedback from the group is essential to make sure you are all on the same track. And while it is important in most cross-cultural groups not to single out individuals to give you this feedback, you can probably recognize or appoint group leaders to speak on behalf of the others.

Flexibility

It is possible to put participants into a simulation whose form or content is virtually guaranteed to alienate them from the start. A good example would be to introduce a simulation game requiring very individualistic behaviour from a group of highly peer-oriented teenagers. Don't make things more difficult for yourself by choosing a game unsuited to the personality of the group, on the dubious grounds that it has always been effective in the past – past circumstances may have been completely different.

An example comes again from our experience of working in PNG. At the University of PNG in Port Moresby we ran a bargaining simulation for local undergraduate business students – a game we describe in Chapter 3 as GOING FINISH. It simulates telephone bargaining by placing participants where they can hear but not see each other. At first we did as we had always done and seated players in pairs, back to back – without realizing how alien a task we were setting for people whose culture is primarily face to face. They could cope with not being able to see the person they were talking to, but not with facing in opposite directions. Though most of them overcame the problem by twisting round in their chairs we could have avoided it altogether by seating each pair face to face, with some kind of screen between them.

Prejudice

If there is cultural, national or any other kind of special prejudice between participants, this can lead to aggression within the playing group that you may not feel comfortable to deal with – yet must learn to handle.

An example is an English-language programme we designed for adult migrants in Australia. Originally from France, Germany, Greece, Italy, Latin America and Lebanon, they now lived in various locations throughout Australia. They had come together in this seminar to improve their English and to practise how to negotiate various social, financial and employment dilemmas. A major drawback was that some students wouldn't even sit next to each other – Jews and Arabs, for example – much less agree to roleplay together. We have also come across this problem with other mixed groups, for example including Japanese and Koreans, Thais and Indians, blacks and whites.

The particular group we are discussing made their ethnic prejudices plain, and matters came to a head when a French-Canadian girl flatly refused, to the silent embarrassment of the class, to join a group which contained a Lebanese man. On the principle of grasping the nettle to draw the sting, we praised her behaviour as demonstrating the need for cross-cultural tolerance in multicultural workplaces. We picked on a couple of Italians whom we already knew to be extrovert and uninhibited, and encouraged them to improvise a dialogue, as follows:

Us: Tony, do you remember telling us about the first time you went to work on a construction site and your Australian workmates laughed at your lunch box?

Tony: Oh, sure I remember, they rubbished me good.

Us: Steffo, if you were a dinkum Aussie, what would you have said to Toni?

Steffo (entering instantly into the spirit of the thing): That you' lunch? What you call that muck, mate?

Toni (likewise): Mate, this olives, this salami . . .

Steffo: You eat that muck? Mate, you gotta be joking. Look, everybody, what this wog eat. Why don't you eat the nice Vegemite sandwich like good Aussie eat?

Toni: Yuk, mate, that stuff taste horrible.

Steffo: You insult our food, mate? I punch-a you' face!

Toni: You punch-a my face, I punch-a you' Vegemite.

A popular car bumper sticker at the time was: 'You smash-a my ute [utility truck, often very old and battered, driven by many

Italian workmen] I punch-a your face'. The sticker was a sly reference to the belief held by many native-born Australians that all Italians drive badly and aggressively. Vegemite, which is a sandwich spread somewhat similar to Marmite, seems to be regarded by Australians as a cultural symbol almost on a par with the national flag. Foreigners and immigrants find this very funny, especially as Vegemite is certainly not to everybody's taste.

Granted this particular ethnic context, it was not surprising that at this point in the improvisation even the Canadian girl was laughing. In the resulting good-humoured atmosphere – which gave these non-Australians the chance to laugh at the locals for a change instead of the other way about – it became easier to discuss prejudice in general and for participants to make real efforts in the following weeks to work together to achieve the objectives of the workshop.

However, some people are so deeply prejudiced against other social groups that nothing will change their minds. Don't assume that every game you direct will change players' behaviour dramatically for the 'better'. You may be the most persuasive leader since the Pied Piper but there are some groups no music will move. One time we directed a simulation game for young players in a corrective institution. We designed a 'cops and robbers' scenario in an attempt to dissipate some of the anti-police prejudice felt by these adolescent boys and to help them negotiate between their peer-group standards and more conventional social behaviour. The results were possibly cathartic for the players in that they released a considerable amount of aggression (the weapons were water-pistols, confetti to simulate tear-gas or mace, and rolled-up newspapers). The resulting mess was indescribable. The players cleaned everything up afterwards with great goodwill, if not competence. Nevertheless, their prejudice against the police remained intact.

Sceptics

Some participants show intolerance to people who don't do things 'their way'; or they have trouble communicating with people outside their own field; or they experience feelings of discomfort in ambiguous or unpredictable situations. These feelings can cause participants to discount game behaviour as meaningless outside its context (which admittedly can sometimes be the case). Also, they may be uncomfortable when asked to discuss their feelings about what happened in the game because they are unused to experiential methods of data collection and consider feelings to be irrelevant to 'facts'. With participants who own this learning style we find it effective to recount similar results evoked by previous game sessions. Quoting chapter and verse often impresses the sceptics sufficiently to persuade them to reconsider the whole experience. However, it is important to remember that all clients should be offered 'hard' as well as 'soft' evidence of a game's effectiveness.

In summary, these then are the major problems you are likely to run up against in multicultural settings:

- attempts by native English speakers to dominate the group through superior language ability;
- the need to cast class-conscious players (and their fellow-nationals) in socially appropriate roles;
- the need to avoid putting participants into culturally alien simulations and to be aware in general of the cultural sensibilities of participants with educational, cultural, national or other background different from your own;
- the existence among group members of cultural, national or other special prejudice;
- the intolerance of some participants for others who don't do things 'their way'; and the difficulty some participants may experience when trying to communicate with people outside their own field, or in ambiguous situations.

Having given all these warnings, we should end by emphasizing again the rewards of simulation in multicultural groups and international settings. In our experience, which we can claim without immodesty to be considerable, participants in these circumstances are likely to be more cooperative, more responsive, less inhibited and more receptive to new ideas than in any other context. Simulation is the ideal teaching method for groups whose members may have language barriers to communication and provides the most effective method we have come across for revealing cultural differences in constructive ways that reduce dissonance and promote mutual respect.

Part II
Activities

Chapter 2
Focus Games

The following is a collection of games, exercises and discussion-starters that illustrate various aspects of negotiation theory. They are all lighthearted and guaranteed to amuse participants as well as stimulate their thinking. They are quite short (none takes longer than an hour to play and debrief), and therefore useful as warm-up activities. Most of them (not all) require very little in the way of special materials or space.

We call this collection 'focus games' because they draw attention to the basic characteristics of negotiation as a process.

- Negotiation involves two or more parties. Even when you negotiate with yourself – for example to decide whether you will go to the cinema or stay home and watch television – you have to assume at least two roles in turn, of protagonist and antagonist respectively.
- Negotiating parties need each other's involvement to achieve some jointly desired outcome. There is no point in negotiating with somebody if they have nothing you want, or you have nothing to offer in return.
- Negotiation is a process for the joint settlement of differences. If you are in complete agreement with the other party there is nothing to negotiate.
- The parties must consider negotiation – at least to start with – to be the most satisfactory way of resolving their differences. Otherwise there will be avoidance, capitulation, legal action or war.
- Each party must believe there is some possibility of persuading the other to modify their original position and agree to a mutually acceptable compromise.
- Each party must have *some* degree of power over the other: if

power is entirely in the hands of one party they may feel no need to negotiate.

- Negotiation is a process primarily of interpersonal communication. However impersonal and corporate the negotiation may be, the human element is always there. The whole range of emotion – pride, anger, humour, fear, acquisitiveness, generosity, antagonism, affection, competitiveness and cooperation – is an essential component in all negotiation.

Thus, we have grouped the first set of focus games in this chapter under the heading of human relations.

Human relations

The first game in this set is a very short activity to put participants into a frame of mind where the above considerations will have real meaning for them. It is particularly suitable as a warm-up to a conference or training course.

GETTING THERE

Objectives:

- to emphasize that all negotiation is a process of human interaction;
- to help participants recognize their own value system. What kind of concessions are they prepared to make? Beyond what concession will they refuse to go?
- to draw participants' attention to the need for alternative strategies in negotiation: the need to have a back-up plan;
- to demonstrate the high mutual benefits of cooperation and joint problem-solving compared to conflict.

Time required: about ten minutes actually to play the game, and about half an hour to discuss it.
Number of players: at least ten: the more the merrier.
Materials: you need a large clear space for this game. If your usual classroom is full of tables and chairs that are difficult to stack, you will have to find somewhere else on this occasion. If you are at a conference, say in a hotel, you can usually find a vacant room that

doesn't have too much furniture. The game is not usually very noisy (though groups vary a lot, particularly across nationalities and cultures) so you could possibly use a corridor, foyer, or even a garden.

Roles: if you are working with large numbers, break them up into groups of about ten people. Tell everybody this is a competitive game between two teams to find out which displays the more efficient teamwork. Pick two team leaders in each group. If you only have about ten players of course there will be only one group of two teams with five people in each. If you know the players individually, choose assertive leaders, preferably two people with very different temperaments. If you are working with strangers, allocate the roles to a man and a woman in each group and select people you think look assertive (how you judge this is up to you!)

Ask leaders to gather their teams, each leader taking it in turn to pick a member. If there is an uneven number of people in a group the odd one will act as observer, but keep an eye on this process – don't let some poor soul get left as an observer by default. If you note that one group is uneven, ask before the selection begins for one volunteer as an observer.

Rules: when all groups have their two teams, tell the leaders in each group to form their respective teams up in two lines, facing each other, with the leaders at the heads of their respective lines. Explain that first the leader in each line, then everybody else in turn, has to cross over to the tail end of the opposite line. The first team to complete this process will be the winner. Then call: 'Ready, steady, GO!' and let them get on with it.

Notes for discussion

It is inevitable that collisions will occur as people cross with each other to get to their respective places in the lines. Observe how and why, and what styles of aggression and avoidance the leaders and team members displayed. When you debrief this behaviour, do so in a context of discussion of the essentials of negotiation as described above. If you're lucky (from a teaching point of view) there may have been some quite rough behaviour during the game, in which case you can point out that negotiation is not always a successful method of achieving compromise: some negotiations fail and the result may be war.

You might also want to remind players of the need to have an alternative strategy in mind in case one's original plans prove unworkable. For example, your presence as game director can provide such an alternative. You are the umpire, the ultimate arbitrator of game behaviour: it is likely that people will ask you (in hope or fear) whether pushing and shoving is allowed, or turn to you for a ruling.

In real life the use of disinterested outside 'experts' might be one method of avoiding stalemate, and you can point this out if players cast you in this role. Another method might be an offer of some form of compensation as a consolation to one party for not getting what they want. You will probably find yourself providing this kind of compensation in the way you praise the losers for being good sports, for example. In the final analysis, however, negotiators need to face up to the question: 'What will I really lose if I walk away (from the table, or the fight)?' The degree of importance to them of the answer will effectively indicate the 'bottom line' of their priorities.

NO MAYBE

This is another game that can serve as an icebreaker or introduction to a conference, seminar or course on negotiating with people from another nationality or culture. Specifically, the content of this exercise relates to negotiations with the Japanese but you can extend its 'messages' when debriefing participants to include virtually any cross-cultural setting.

Objectives:

- to gain insights into cross-cultural communication;
- to learn to paraphrase and re-word messages more appropriately for the people who are to receive them;
- to acquire cultural sensitivity.

Time: about half an hour, including debriefing.
Number of players: any number. Large groups can be divided into sub-groups and they can compare notes afterwards.
Materials: preferably a gong or a pair of cymbals. If you can't get hold of anything like these, try and find something that makes a similar kind of noise. A metal spoon hitting a tin tray should be effective.

The game: with the exception of two players, organize everybody into a circle or circles – about five to ten people in each circle. Give one reserved player the gong. Give the other the list of questions below. Explain to the players in the circle that the rule of the game is that they are to evade a direct answer to any questions put to them. How they do this is up to them, but they cannot use any evasion that has been used by a previous speaker. If they do, or if they do not evade the question, they will be 'gonged' out of the game.

The following are some sample questions. You may have to ask them yourself if you are short of players; and of course you can ask the same question more than once. If you ask the questions yourself the person who bangs the gong must be the umpire.

- What is your name? (An evasive answer might be: 'When I got married I changed my name, so that's a hard question to answer ...'.)
- What kind of transport did you use to get here? (example of evasive answer: 'It depends whether you mean private or public transport.')
- Do you have a driving licence? ('I'll tell you if you tell me.')
- What kind of music do you like? ('That's too personal a question.')
- Can you recall the colour of your mother's eyes?
- Do you feel you should lose some weight?
- What school did you go to?
- How many brothers and sisters have you?
- Where do you live?
- Where do you work?

Note that all these questions are specific; and some of them are quite beguiling – that is, people find it difficult not to answer them directly. You may find one or two people remain in the game long after the others have dropped out. Continue to ask them questions until either you or they get tired of the game.

Notes for debriefing*

Summarize the strategies, tactics and manoeuvres people employed to evade the questions. Note whether the range was

* Adapted from Graham and Sano 1984:24

large or small (how long was it before every player was gonged out?) Then share with them the following ways by which the Japanese commonly avoid saying no:

- a vague and ambiguous yes or no (as in 'Well, I suppose it might be so ...');
- silence;
- counter-question;
- tangential response (as in 'When you ask about my mother, I'm not sure how to answer, since my father was married three times ...');
- walking out;
- telling lies or making excuses;
- criticizing the question;
- refusing the question;
- making the no conditional (as in 'I shall have to answer no to that question because of the way the question is phrased, though I don't necessarily agree with it.' Or 'I will answer that question only if you first answer a question from me.');
- saying 'yes, but ...' (and then qualifying the answer so as to render it virtually meaningless);
- delaying an answer (as in 'We will write you a letter.');
- making an apology.

You will probably find that at least one player will try to use rudeness as a tactic – for example by answering a question with some version of 'Mind your own business!' Allow this (though only one player in a circle can be permitted to refuse outright to answer). Point out afterwards how crass a response insult is, compared to the more subtle examples above; and initiate a discussion on the gentle art of prevarication. This game can provide players with valuable practice in diplomacy, or help to prepare them for a political career!

CHAIN OF COMMAND

A game about joint problem-solving as a negotiation strategy.

This is a competitive game to study the problem-solving behaviour of effective teams. It sets competing teams to solve a puzzle that requires close cooperation between respective team members.

Objectives:

- to suggest that every member has a uniquely important contribution to make to a team effort. The contribution may be of special knowledge, effective communication, a sense of common purpose, the creation of good relationships, infectious enthusiasm, or anything else;
- to demonstrate the importance of good relationships within negotiating groups and a sense of common purpose;
- to illustrate the effects on negotiation of joint problem-solving behaviour by all parties;
- to emphasize the coordinating role of leaders of negotiating teams.

Time: about an hour.

Number of players: CHAIN OF COMMAND can be played with a minimum of five players; for maximum effect, there should be at least two teams in competition, ie a minimum of ten players. Virtually any number above ten can play, in groups of about five people each.

Materials:

- a room large enough for players to move around freely;
- a desk, table, whatever, at which the team leader can work;
- instruction cards for each team member of each group;
- instruction cards for the two players in each team who take the respective roles of CEO (chief executive officer, or senior manager) and team leader;
- material for creating a picture in several colours. This can be a large sheet of art cardboard and a set of felt-tipped pens; a whiteboard and set of markers; a blackboard and coloured chalks; or a graphics package and computer. Game instructions are for the colours red, black, blue, green, yellow. If other colours are used, the instructions will need to be amended accordingly. If cardboard is used, the game director may like to include a long ruler, protractor, compasses, etc, but these are optional extras.

The game: explain to everybody the object of the game is to help the team leader to create a picture according to certain criteria. The first team whose leader completes the task will be the winner. Team leaders cannot make their pictures until they have all the necessary information that only their team members can provide. The CEO's role is to provide artistic direction.

Roles: if there are more than five players, divide them into at least two groups with the following composition:

- one CEO, whose business is to decide the artistic and other standards to which the team product must comply;
- one team leader, who has to coordinate the combined information from all team members in order to compose a picture;
- at least three, preferably five or more, team members. The more team members, the more complex the task becomes. Team members have to supply the leader with essential information on how to create the picture.

Action: label each player clearly as CEO, Team Leader, Team Member A, B, C, etc.

Introduce each role in turn, so that everybody knows who everybody is and what they are supposed to be doing. Distribute the instruction cards and tell everybody they can start when they are ready. The instructions below assume five team members.

After you have explained the game and distributed the role cards take no further part in the game. When a team announces the task has been completed, check that all criteria have been met. If not, ask the players to finish it, but do not tell them yet what the omissions are – let them try to work these out for themselves.

Notes for debriefing

When the game is over, help players to assess the extent to which joint problem-solving led to high mutual benefits. What kind of leadership style did the leaders display? What kind of teamwork appeared to be most effective?

Instructions for team leader

Your task is to compose a picture with as much artistry as you can, under certain constraints. You have to work out what these constraints are, from information provided by your team. When you think you have all the information you need, create your artwork, under the final supervision of your CEO. The following materials have been provided for you: some kind of 'canvas' on which to create your picture, and colouring utensils in red, black, blue, green and yellow.

Instructions for CEO

You are in artistic control of a picture that the team leader will compose. Within the constraints that will appear during the course of the game you must ensure the finished picture conforms to your artistic and professional standards.

Instructions for team member A

You have important information for your team leader, without which the group task cannot be completed. This is your information:

$$18 - HXs = 9A + Bs = 11(2)Xs$$

However, you have to understand what it means before you can pass it on. To do this you need other team members' special knowledge – and they need yours.

Your special knowledge is that: M means one; H means two; S means three; 18 means four. As soon as you have decoded your information with the help of your colleagues, take it to your team leader.

Instructions for team member B

You have important information for your team leader, without which the group task cannot be completed. This is your information:

$$4M(5)(10)22H(2)Xs + 18Bs = 11(5)(10)$$

However, you have to understand what it means before you can pass it on. To do this you need other team members' special knowledge – and they need yours. Your special knowledge is that: (2) means red; (5) means blue; C means black; 19 means green; 18 means yellow. As soon as you have decoded your information with the help of your colleagues, take it to your team leader.

Instructions for team member C

You have important information for your team leader, without which the group task cannot be completed. This is your information:

$$H(2)Xs = 12MC23 + 4MC13 \ 12M(2)X$$

However, you have to understand what it means before you can pass it on. To do this you need other team members' special knowledge – and they need yours. Your special knowledge is that: B means pentagon (Bs is the plural); 13 means hexagon; P means cross; 23 means triangle; (10) means circle; X means oblong (Xs is the plural); E means eye. As soon as you have decoded your information with the help of your colleagues, take it to your team leader.

Instructions for team member D

You have important information for your team leader, without which the group task cannot be completed. This is your information:

$$4M19E \ 12MX + 18Bs > (5)(10)$$

However, you have to understand what it means before you can pass it on. To do this you need other team members' special knowledge – and they need yours. Your special knowledge is that: 12 means inside; 11 means outside; 22 means between; > means is or are larger than; 9 means on top of; 4 means there is or there are; A means each other. As soon as you have decoded your information with the help of your colleagues, take it to your team leader.

Instructions for team member E

You have important information for your team leader, without which the group task cannot be completed. This is your information:

$$S18Bs = 12C23 + 4M(2)P \ 12M \ 18B$$

However, you have to understand what it means before you can pass it on. To do this you need other team members' special knowledge – and they need yours. Your special knowledge is that:

- means subtract; + means and; = means are. As soon as you have decoded your information with the help of your colleagues, take it to your team leader.

Confidential checklist for game director: summary of instructions for the picture, with the respective codes, their meanings, and which team member has which coded instruction

The finished picture should contain the following. Make sure all criteria have been met before accepting a finished product:

- Two oblongs, one above the other (literally: '4 minus 2 oblongs are on top of each other'). The code for this instruction is: 18-HXs = 9A, held by team member A.
- A blue circle between the two oblongs, which are red (literally: 'there is one blue circle between two red oblongs'). 4M(5)(10)22H(2)Xs: team member B.
- The two oblongs are contained within a black triangle (literally: 'two red oblongs are inside one black triangle'). H(2)Xs = 12MC23: team member C.
- Literally: 'there is one green eye inside one oblong'. 4M19E 12MX: team member D.
- The triangle also contains three yellow pentagons (literally: 'three yellow pentagons are inside black triangle'. S18Bs = 12C23: team member E.
- Literally: 'pentagons are outside red oblongs'. Bs = 11(2)Xs: team member A
- 'Yellow pentagons are outside blue circle'. 18Bs = 11(5)(10): team member B
- 'There is one black hexagon inside one red oblong'. 4MC13 12M(2)X: team member C
- 'Yellow pentagons are larger than blue circle'. 18Bs > (5)(10): team member D
- 'There is one red cross inside one yellow pentagon'. 4M(2)P 12 M 18 B: team member E

All the above information should be shared with the players when the game is over.

The code

Also to be shared with the players in debriefing.

Code	Real meaning
M	one
H	two
S	three
18	four
(2)	red
(5)	blue
C	black
19	green
18	yellow
B	pentagon
Bs	pentagons
13	hexagon
P	cross
23	triangle
(10)	circle
X	oblong
Xs	oblongs
E	eye
12	inside
11	outside
22	between
>	are larger than
9	on top of
4	there is or there are
A	each other
–	subtract
+	and
=	are

FOUR LETTER WORDS

This game demonstrates that negotiation requires intense verbal, personal and social interactions on individual and group levels: individual in the sense of person-to-person transactions in a variety of roles; group to the extent that each side has a collective style and set of attitudes of its own. The good negotiator has either an intuitive or a trained ability to sense the changing moods and concerns of individuals and groups and to adopt appropriate behaviour to influence them.

Objectives:

- to demonstrate how the attitudes of individuals can affect negotiation outcomes;
- to illustrate that individual perceptions of what a negotiation is 'really' about will vary widely from person to person;
- to suggest that control of negotiation outcomes will depend to a large extent on the degree to which one party can affect the other's perceptions and attitudes towards the negotiation.

Time: about an hour.

Number of participants: any number, in small groups of five to seven people.

Materials: prepare two envelopes for each group, each containing ten letters of the alphabet. Tell players that one envelope contains letters from the first half of the alphabet and mostly vowels; and the other one contains letters from the second half of the alphabet and mostly consonants.

Scenario, roles and rules: Divide people into small groups of five to seven people and give a set of two envelopes, prepared as above, to each group. Each group elects a leader. The task is to decide which envelope to open (with unlimited time for discussion) and then to make as many words as possible from the letters in two minutes.

Notes for debriefing

Four major aspects of negotiation are its purpose, its process, the ideas generated during the process, and the relationships that develop between the parties. Thus negotiation is concerned with four kinds of behaviour orientation: task, process, ideas and people. By temperament, genetic inheritance, professional background and training – and no doubt for many more reasons – most people tend to have a stronger orientation towards one of these behaviours than the others, though everybody is capable of all four.

Thus if one member of a negotiating team is strongly affiliative in temperament, they are likely to serve the team best by concentrating on achieving as good a relationship as possible between team members and between the negotiating parties. They might be given the responsibility, for example, of finding a congenial meeting place, of organizing the refreshments; or they might be asked to act as go-between in the initial stages, and so on.

FOUR LETTER WORDS evokes these four behaviours from players in the following ways:

- Some people will be more interested in the *affiliative* aspects of the game, the fun of being part of a group activity, the relaxation of discussion relatively free from time constraints, the intellectual stimulus of listening to viewpoints other than their own, and so on. Such participants are not particularly interested in choosing an envelope: in fact sometimes they will say straight out they don't think it's important to open an envelope at all – making words out of letters is not what they see the game as being 'about'.

- Others see the game quite differently: they press *to get on with the task* and emphasize that the group should choose an envelope as soon as possible.

- Others again are *process-minded*. It is important to these people to plan which envelope to open, which letters would be more useful, what words can be formed.

- Meanwhile there will almost always be a minority of players more interested in *ideas* than interaction or process. 'Ideas people' like to deal in concepts. For example, are vowels really more useful than consonants in forming words?

When you debrief players after FOUR LETTER WORDS you might also like to include the following observations about the kinds of behaviour which not only are non-productive in negotiation but actually tend to alienate the other party (and probably one's own team members as well):

- Excessive use of the first person singular. If you continually say: 'I think we should . . .' or 'I don't want to . . .', a common reaction, spoken or unspoken is: 'Who does s/he think s/he is? S/he's not the leader of this game!'

- Personal criticism of other people, such as: 'Why are you wasting so much time? Why don't you open the envelope and get on with it?' More constructive approaches in negotiation are to listen, question and summarize.
- Point-scoring for the fun of it, for example: 'If we had planned this more carefully to start with, as I suggested . . .' If people really feel the need to say something like this, they could follow it with a more positive suggestion, such as: 'But we can still do such-and-such . . .'
- Allocating blame, as: 'You were the one who was in such a hurry . . .' instead of remaining objective and impersonal.
- Frequently interrupting other people, making too much eye contact with them and speaking in too loud a voice, are all aggressive verbal and non-verbal behaviours. A more positive and effective behaviour in negotiation is to persuade rather than bully.

OTTO'S GAME

This game is about relationships. Negotiation is likely to be more effective if the participants understand and respect each other's strengths, even if they don't like each other. The objective is not to form personal friendships – though if this happens, it is no bad thing. What is needed is a sound trading relationship, without false bonhomie or patronising behaviour. Much of the power and influence of a good negotiating team stems from members' confidence in each other – a confidence based on shared information and knowledge of those aspects of each other's personality that together make a winning combination.

The game illustrates how such a combination emerges as survival of the fittest in a competitive environment. We call it OTTO'S GAME because it was given to us by Otto van Veen of the Management Development Centre in Mijgnrode, the Netherlands.

Objectives:

- to demonstrate effective relationships in negotiation teams;
- to reproduce the selection processes that occur during the development of effective negotiation teams;
- to illustrate some of the constraints that operate on these selection processes.

Time required: about an hour.

Number of participants: any number can play, but you will have to divide large groups into smaller syndicates for convenience.

Materials:

- a pack of cards for each playing group;
- the same amount of money for each player in each playing group. We use real money because it seems to add value to the game but if you are playing with large numbers you may have to use toy money. If you have real currency, give each player the equivalent of about one pound sterling or one US or Australian dollar in small change.

Scenario: OTTO'S GAME is played in as many rounds as you want, as follows:

- Each player contributes about 10p to the kitty, held by the banker (you, unless you can get somebody else to fill this role).
- The banker has one or more packs of cards, depending on the number of players.
- Each player is dealt five free cards. The remainder of the pack is then placed on the table.
- Players may pick up and discard cards, always retaining five cards in their hand, but they have to buy the new cards at 10p each. Their objective is to assemble as high a score as possible, as follows:

    Jack = 11; queen = 12; king = 13; ace = 14; joker = 0.

All other cards have their face value.

- When everybody is satisfied (or after about three minutes), negotiation begins. All players have to join one of two coalitions. Any combination of players is allowed, but if there are many people in one coalition, individual winnings in that coalition will be small.
- The banker pays the difference between the lower and the higher score to the winning coalition: that is, the highest five-card score from the combined hands of the coalition members. Members then divide their winnings equally, and the next round begins. Round 2 is the same as Round 1. Players who lose all their

money quit the game. Play at least three or four hands. Don't worry if these instructions sound complicated – there may be some initial confusion among players during the first round but after that everybody will understand the game.

Notes for debriefing

There are two group impulses here: to avoid having somebody with a low score in your group; and to join up with a few select people who have high scores, whether your own is low or high. Thus players have an irresistible urge to form relationships with a few people who can contribute substantially to the coalition. Such contribution consists of more than money – because successful players will be those who are quick-witted enough to draw and discard cards in high-score combinations. These are the players who will woo other high-scorers to their side, and be wooed by them. Because an individual can't beat the group, it becomes important for players to join the right group. As one player put it to us: 'Everybody wants to know you if you've got something they want. Nobody wants to know you if you've got nothing they want.'

Logically, each group should consist of five people to maximize profits. Therefore some larger groups will reject their surplus members – some groups throw out all members who have contributed no cards to the final collective hand. You may want to ask rejected players how they feel.

Some groups seem more willing than others to tolerate their non-productive members, and it is interesting to discuss this. Why are some teams more people-minded and others more task-oriented? One answer you are likely to receive from the people-oriented groups is that members like each other, feel comfortable together, and therefore gamble on the assumption that the people with low scores will pick up a better hand in the next round.

OTTO'S GAME is a useful activity for cross-cultural groups because it gives them the opportunity afterwards to broaden the discussion into a debate about the extent to which different cultures are or are not prepared to support their non-contributing members. For example, as a result of playing OTTO'S GAME we have found ourselves debating the entire concept of a state welfare system.

ROSEMARY'S RIVER

Fowler (1986) is one of many writers to point out that a general rule of negotiation is to avoid becoming emotionally committed – bargainers need cool heads and an objective outlook. If you want to demonstrate how personal feelings affect people's judgment, and therefore their negotiation priorities, the following short exercises may serve your purpose. Both stories have the advantage that they will elicit value-judgments – that is, emotional responses – from participants without their getting offensively personal with each other. Don't be tempted to think these exercises are simplistic. They may be simple, but you will find that quite complex emotions and strongly felt arguments develop from them – which is what you want to happen, in order to demonstrate how subjective is most people's 'reality'.

Time required: about 20 minutes to three-quarters of an hour, depending on the size of the group.

Participants: any number can play this game. Divide large groups into syndicates and hold a plenary session afterwards to compare notes. However if you have to do this, make sure you've appointed a good storyteller to each group, and that these narrators have been well briefed.

Materials: a blackboard, whiteboard or flipchart on which to draw Rosemary's river and indicate where the characters in the story are located in relation to it.

Scenario: draw two wavy lines on the board a few inches apart and announce that this is a river. Write the names Fred, Rosemary and Sinbad well spaced along one bank of the river; write the names Geoffrey and Dennis somewhere along the opposite bank. Tell the following story and ask participants to make notes.

> Rosemary is a poor girl from a poor country who is engaged to marry a rich foreigner, Geoffrey. In order to wed him she has to cross the water. She has no means of transport but Sinbad has a boat so she asks him to ferry her over. Sinbad agrees, but only on condition that she have sex with him. Rosemary refuses, and asks Fred to help her. Fred is sympathetic but says he can't help. Finally, Rosemary agrees to Sinbad's bargain and has sex with him. Sinbad then ferries her across the river. When Rosemary is united with Geoffrey she confesses what has happened. Geoffrey refuses to marry her.

Dennis then offers to marry her, though he tells her he doesn't love her.

When you have told this story, ask your listeners to agree upon the answers to the following questions:

- Who behaved most creditably and why?
- Who behaved least creditably and why?
- What should Rosemary do now?
- What is the story really about?

Notes for debriefing

We are always surprised, when we tell this story, by the range of responses we get; for example:

- Sinbad is the villain, Dennis is the hero. Rosemary should count herself lucky and marry Dennis.
- Rosemary behaved least creditably because she passively allowed people to exploit her. Geoffrey is the hero because of his high moral principles. Rosemary should learn to stand up for herself.
- Fred is the villain because he refused to help a damsel in distress. Sinbad behaved creditably because his behaviour was totally pragmatic. Rosemary should marry Sinbad.
- Geoffrey is the villain for throwing Rosemary over. Rosemary was the heroine because she tried so hard to join her lover. Her loyalty will no doubt be rewarded in time because if she is patient Geoffrey will forgive her.

As advocates of women's liberation from the traditional stereotypes that constrain and demean them, some participants find themselves appalled by some of these (often passionately spoken) statements, which illustrate that listeners' reactions to the story are the point of this exercise. The story seems always to be interpreted quite differently by different people, depending on their subjective frame of reference - which in turn will provoke emotional replies. As for what the story is 'really' about, for some people it stands as a metaphor for the Third World trying to achieve First World standards. For others it identifies the problems women face in trying to achieve more power and status.

Others hear it more abstractly as a problem-solving or negotiation exercise – though even these more objective listeners usually include some kind of value-judgement.

Towards the end of the discussion you can compare the divergence in participants' views with the different viewpoints of, say, union representatives and management over industrial relations isssues. Ask for suggestions about how to defuse emotion in order to find some consensus among the negotiators on what the problem really is about.

Below is another version of the story, which raises different issues.

DAVID'S DILEMMA

David is in love with Daphne who lives on a tiny island called Pacifica under the high mountain Sim Sala, which is subject to volcanic eruptions. One day Daphne telephones David in a panic because lava is pouring from the mountain and the whole island is in danger. As she speaks the line goes dead and David knows there is no time to lose. He runs down the road to Dana, who owns a boatshed. Dana has been hopelessly in love with David for years and now proposes they strike a sexual bargain over the boat. David refuses angrily and hunts all over the area to find another boat but they are all out on the rescue operation to save the island. However, David doesn't dare leave it to chance that his beloved will be among the rescued. He returns to Dana and agrees to the bargain – which means nothing to him emotionally, though this is the most wonderful experience of Dana's life. Then David takes the boat and motors to the island. When he gets there he finds everybody celebrating because the volcano has become dormant again. David tells Daphne of his valiant struggle to reach her, and the sacrifice of his honour. She is horrified and refuses to have anything more to do with him. David is heartbroken.

When you have told this story, ask your listeners:

- Who is the most moral (or high-principled) person in the story?
- What should David do now?

Let the discussion run on until one or more people have

expressed sympathy for Dana and perhaps have suggested that she and David might console each other. Then say, with an air of slight surprise: 'Oh, no, Dana isn't a woman, he's a man'; and see what happens.

The point of the story, from your perspective, is that it illustrates how a situation can suddenly seem quite different when assumptions based on value-judgments are challenged. How do people negotiate with a perceived discrepancy between expectations and reality – known as cognitive dissonance? How can the answers to these and similar questions be related to real-life negotiation?

LISTENING

Learning to listen to what the other party is really saying is an essential negotiation skill. In fact, the most common fault in negotiating may be to talk too much and listen too little. This may not be as important during the first phase of negotiation, if this consists of each side stating its own position in a fairly aggressive way. But once a collaborative phase is reached, the search is on for common ground and acceptable compromise. This is when listening assumes top priority and experienced negotiators switch from making statements to asking questions and then listening carefully to the answers. Moreover, a question from one party may be answered by another question from the other party, not to score points but to increase the amount and quality of feedback. For example, a union representative may ask a management delegate: 'Is there any chance of your changing your minds on the issue of working hours?' To which management might reply: 'Can you explain why you seem to be giving this item such a high priority?' Thus debate is enlarged and the possibility increased that each side will understand the other's point of view.

LISTENING demonstrates that listening by itself is not enough. Communication is a two-way process in which the message-sender must have feedback from the receiver to make sure the message has been understood as intended. It is based on a game by John Sleigh, from his book *Making Learning Fun* (1989), adapted with his permission.

Objectives: to illustrate the need for feedback from people working under instruction, to make sure they understand what it is they have to do.

Time: about half an hour.

Number of players: any number.

Setting and roles: participants are given a series of apparently simple instructions without feedback on their progress as they carry out them out.

1. Give a blank sheet of paper to each participant.
2. Tell everybody the game is so simple they can do it with their eyes shut. Then ask them to close their eyes (or you can blindfold them, depending on number of players and if time and numbers warrant it).
3. Make sure their eyes are closed, then ask them to fold the sheet of paper. Don't answer any questions – tell them the rules don't allow it.
4. Say: 'Tear the top right-hand corner.'
5. Say: 'Fold the sheet of paper.'
6. 'Tear the bottom left-hand corner.'
7. 'Fold the sheet of paper.'
8. 'Tear the top left-hand corner.'
9. 'Before you open your eyes, raise your hand if you have followed all the instructions.'
10. 'Open your eyes and check with the person next to you, whether or not your sheets are identical. If they are not, raise your hands.'

It is very rare for any two sheets to be so similar that they can fairly be called identical.

Notes for debriefing

Ask everybody what was missing from the communication process they went through. The answer, of course, is feedback. Was it evident to most of them immediately that lack of feedback would lead to problems with task accomplishment? How can we ensure as far as possible that the 'messages' we send in the negotiation process are received as intended?

BLUEPRINT

Casse and Deol (1985:80) in their excellent book on managing intercultural negotiations, suggest that planning (along with decision-making, conflict resolution and teamwork) is a key characteristic of negotiating styles. They identify four kinds of planners: those who focus on the present, the here and now; those who focus on the future, on short-, medium- or long-term interests; those who relate past and present to future; and those who focus on the past.

The effectiveness of BLUEPRINT is in its capacity to help players begin to recognize their negotiating strengths as planners. The original game was given to us by our friend the late Dr Barry Moore of Sydney, Australia. The scenario of BLUEPRINT is one in which teams of players, each under the direction of a supervisor, compete against each other to build a model in the shortest reasonable time. However, the game is designed to create conflict between short-term and long-term planners, to isolate and identify their respective priorities. Then, in discussion after the game, players compare and contrast their negotiation behaviour with the objective of making it more effective in the sense of being appropriate to the situation in which it is located.

Time required: about an hour.
Number of players: any number, divided into small groups.
Materials: you can use the same game kit for BLUEPRINT as for MRP (Chapter 4), which consists of building materials and a blueprint. If you don't have it, you can use drawing pins and drinking straws; Lego bricks; cardboard, scissors and staples; or any other set of building materials and a plan of a model that can be built with them. Any large toy shop sells building models of this kind; but if you are a handyperson who enjoys elementary carpentry you can make your own kit, for example with the following components for four groups, each of three people (12 players in all):

- 320 wooden ice-cream spoons, each with a small hole drilled at each end (80 per group of four people);
- four small screwdrivers (one per group);
- about 700 small screws with washers, to fit the holes in the sticks (175 per group);
- four copies (one per group) of a diagram of how the sticks must be screwed together to make, for instance, the girders and fasteners of a Bailey Bridge.

Action:

1. Divide participants into small groups, each of three to five people.
2. Give each group a copy of the blueprint and the materials to build the model.
3. Tell all groups they have ten minutes to estimate how long, in minutes, it will take them to build the model. They can actually start to build a prototype if they want.
4. After ten minutes, each group must put in a sealed bid (a time estimate) for constructing the model. Each team will be held to its own time estimate.
5. Set a timer or start a clock for the construction phase to begin – which will probably last about 20 minutes.
6. Allow at least one group to complete the task and time how long it took. If any of the other groups are nearly finished, continue to time them; otherwise declare the construction phase over.
7. Open each sealed bid. Post each group's estimated construction time on the board, together with the time it actually took them to complete the model. If any group was not able to complete its model, write a question mark in the appropriate column.
8. Ask all groups to discuss quietly among themselves what they think they did right and what they should have done but did not, to match performance to estimate. Give everybody about five minutes to do this.
9. Call a plenary session and post summaries of each group's deliberations.

Notes for debriefing

You are likely to find that some players will have been more concerned to calculate an accurate estimate than to build the model; others will have been more inclined to guess at the estimate and to concentrate more on the actual model. In other words, some players will be more future- and some more present-oriented. What kind of negotiation did they engage in to complete the exercise? Did some people think it essential to build a prototype? Why?

By asking questions like this, and listening to the answers, you can build reasonably accurate pictures of individual players' planning styles and also the planning style of the group. This brings us to the next set of focus games, dealing with the world of work: labour relations.

Labour relations

LALAIKA

The concept of planning includes that of responsibility. When business companies plan their use of materials and resources (including human resources) and negotiate to acquire them, their responsibilities are not only to be productive and profitable but also to avoid sabotage to the external environment from which their resoures are drawn. Jandt and Gillette (1985) have a good chapter on the adverse effects of conflict within organizations and they are two of many writers who discuss ways to avoid industrial sabotage. But no writer on industrial relations (as far as we know) mentions another form of sabotage - the damage that business organizations can inflict on the wider social environment if they lack a sense of social responsibility in their negotiations with it.

LALAIKA is designed to draw this aspect of negotiation to players' attention. It is a messy game because the players have to shell peanuts; but don't allow this minor problem to deter you. It is very simple to set up, a lot of fun to play, and thought-provoking.

Objectives:

- to demonstrate the impact a business can have on the society in which it operates and with which it has to negotiate in order to keep in business;
- to indicate ways in which the aesthetics and safety of the physical environment will be affected unless this negotiation includes socially responsible behaviour by the organization.

Time: about half an hour.
Number of players: seven to 12 or more players, in at least one group of five, with at least two observers.
Materials:

- a large bag of unshelled peanuts (or any kind of nut) for each team;

- a pair of gloves, preferably heavy gardening gloves, for each player who takes the role of a trainee;
- about ten pounds sterling in 50p coins;
- a book of tear-off tickets (like a book of raffle tickets) to symbolize a cheque book.

Scenario (one copy for each player): senior management at Pacific Peanuts has become frustrated with having to pay high salaries to their home workforce. They have decided to move part of their operation offshore and have chosen, provisionally, the tiny island of Lalaika, whose population includes about 35,000 unskilled young people. Unfortunately, Pacific did not bother to carry out an ETOP (environmental threats and opportunities profile). Pacific sent over a team of trainers to introduce a training programme to groups of young Lalaikans, with the objective of creating a workforce able to perform the value-added operation to their raw food materials (that is, to shell the nuts) at minimal cost.

Roles: players take the roles of supervisors (representatives of Pacific Peanuts); workers (Lalaikans); and observers (overseas consumers). How you introduce the roles is up to you. You may want to set up an exploitative, paternalistic or democratic relationship between the people of Lalaika, or you may prefer to do what we do, which is to allow the relationship to evolve of its own accord depending on the characteristics of the playing group.

Allocate the roles, issue gloves to the workers and while they are putting them on and getting into their groups, have a few words with the observers and supervisors, to agree on the price of the raw materials (the bags of nuts), the selling price of the value-added product (the shelled nuts) and the range of wages the supervisors can pay, from minimum to maximum.

Finalize the teams. Each team will consist of a supervisor from Pacific Peanuts and four local (Lalaikan) workers who will shell the nuts. It is the responsibility of the supervisors to announce the terms and conditions of employment – wages, any penalties for broken or spoiled nuts (if they fall to the floor, for example) and so on.

At the start of the game all the workers will be wearing gloves. The money is divided out between the observers.

Rules: each supervisor buys a bag of peanuts from the supplier (you, unless you can delegate another player to the role). The supervisors pay by 'cheque' and receive a receipt; they then take the bags over to their respective group of workers, who shell the nuts as quickly as they can.

The game is played in at least three rounds, each of ten minutes. Supervisors have to pay wages to the workers at the end of each round (also by cheque), sell the consignment of shelled nuts to the observers and buy more peanuts as required (all these are paper transactions).

At the beginning of each round, after round one, the supervisors can instruct one worker to remove one glove (to symbolize improvement in shelling skills). Eventually, if the game goes on long enough, all the workers will be barehanded.

Also at the beginning of each round, workers can negotiate for more pay, and the supervisors can change the retail price of the nuts (though the customers don't have to buy them if they think the price is too high). The supervisors have to balance their chequebook outgoings against cash received. The supervisor whose team has made the biggest profit wins the game.

Notes for debriefing

1. It is interesting to observe how long the workers refrain from interfering in management. Many players, for example, as soon as they fully understand what the game entails, begin making suggestions to the supervisors to improve profitability. If this happens, how do the supervisors respond? If you have set the game up as a situation of 'us' (the colonizing overlords) and 'them' (the colonized and therefore inferior workers), the supervisors may resent any such intervention. On the other hand, management-worker relations may have been democratic from the start. What comments occur to participants about organizational conflict in this potentially exploitative setting?

2. What has happened to the nutshells? Have players dropped them on the floor, or have they made tidier arrangements? Discuss whatever they did in terms of an organization's environmental responsibilities.

3. You might like to share our paraphrase of some negotiating strategies that Jandt and Gillette (1985) offer to limit the damage and maximize the productivity that can come out of conflicts such as the above:

- The supervisors might have created an organizational climate in which the workers felt free to make suggestions and raise objections. If they did not, did this cause conflict and limit productivity?
- Did supervisors solicit workers' opinions without constraining them by defining the kind of response expected of them? This is argued to be an effective negotiation tactic.
- Was there productive liaison between working groups? Did supervisors consult with each other? Did supervisors consult with customers?

*   *   *

Scott Myers, in *Managing with Unions* (1978:119-123) was one of the first writers on industrial negotiation to point out that there seem to be three models of labour relations:

1. the win-lose adversary model;
2. the collaborative adversary;
3. industrial democracy.

Myers pointed out that win-lose adversary relationships characterize the vast majority of management-union relations; unfortunately, more than a decade later this still seems to be true. Bargainers are taught fine points of debate and legal loopholes; they are briefed on precedents established in other bargaining situations; given insights to the motivational principles underlying their adversary's strategies; updated on the company's financial status and the results of compensation surveys; and generally encouraged to use 'tricks' to win. The result is that people who otherwise would probably harbour no malice towards each other are required by the system to identify themselves as belonging to 'management' or 'labour' and to declare themselves implicitly if not explicitly as enemies.

The following three games focus discussion of these ideas.

WIN-LOSE

You may not want to play this game with students from countries such as Japan, China, Korea, Indonesia, or from any cultural background that is group-orientated rather than assertively individualist. British, European, American or Australian participants should be able to handle it and find it useful.

Announce that this game is about persuasion. Select one member of the group and send that person out of the room. It doesn't matter what the selection process is. If group members are comfortable with each other you will probably get a volunteer; otherwise they can pick a card from a deck, throw a die or whatever is most convenient.

Let us imagine you have sent a woman called Sara out of the room. Seat the rest of the group in chairs in a circle with an empty chair in the middle. Tell them they are going to persuade Sara, when she comes back, to perform a task. The following are some suggestions:

- to pour a glass of water and drink it;
- write something (like the date) on the blackboard;
- shake hands with another group member;
- open or shut a window.

The group should be able to make some suggestions. The only rules are that Sara shall not be required to do anything undignified or unsafe and that she shall not be told the nature of the task until she has completed it. In other words she cannot be asked directly to do whatever it is. Persuasion must be oblique.

When everybody is clear about what they have to do, escort Sara back into the room and seat her in the middle of the circle. Explain to her that she cannot refuse any reasonable request from the group, whether she understands its purpose or not. By this time Sara is probably sitting nervously on the chair, wondering what's going on and suspecting she's going to be made a fool of.

Let's imagine the task is to persuade her to open a window – without asking her directly to do so. A group member might comment on how hot it was and ask somebody else in the circle to open the window. That person refuses and the request goes round the circle. Everybody says no, and they all look expectantly at Sara without saying anything. If Sara feels sufficiently assertive she may look straight back at them without moving, or she may say something like: 'All right, I get the idea!' and go across to open the window.

Another tactic we observed was contained in the following dialogue:

Q: Would you go over to the window, please?

A: I'm at the window, what am I supposed to do now?

Q: What's it like outside?

A: (Begins to describe the view.)

Q: But I need to feel what kind of a day it is out there.

A: I suppose you want me to open the window?

Q: Does it seem to you a reasonable request?

A: (Grudgingly) Yes, I suppose so. (Opens the window.)

Points for discussion

Some groups come up with really ingenious tasks, and some 'volunteers' are very smart at guessing what's expected of them and either cooperating or outwitting the group. Because the group is not allowed to ask the volunteer directly to perform the chosen task, the vital part of their agenda is hidden. An awareness of deception, of something concealed and therefore potentially threatening, communicates itself to the volunteer. Thus the volunteer is likely to feel 'used' after being coerced into doing something s/he probably would have done quite willingly if asked directly, and in which case everybody would have felt OK about the whole transaction.

If you are playing this game to illustrate some aspect of industrial relations you can ask if employees are not in a similar no-win situation when employers do not tell them the strategic purposes of tasks they are required to perform.

COLLABORATIVE ADVERSARY

Myers (1978) argues that collaborative adversary relationships are typified by a state of mutual respect between employer and employee. Each recognizes the other's priorities, for example that the former is concerned primarily with performance, productivity and profit; the latter with satisfaction of material, physical and psychological needs in the workplace. It is recognized by all concerned that these two sets of priorities can coexist peacefully and that both can be achieved through cooperation. The concepts of 'management by objectives' and 'total quality management' are examples of how this can be done, whereby labour–management working parties encourage rank-and-file workers to become involved in decision-making.

You can demonstrate this in game form with large quantities of Lego or any other kind of coloured building blocks, coloured straws, beads, etc. Divide the materials generously among group members so that some have green bricks, straws or beads, some red, some yellow and so on. Then announce that the objective of the game is that each group build a structure in three colours; a winning structure will be selected by you on the criteria of size, stability and beauty. The only rules are that nobody is allowed to talk, and nobody is allowed to beg, borrow or steal anybody else's materials without being offered them.

This almost always turns out to be a peaceful, cooperative activity in which people mutely exchange some colours for others, bargain in pantomime and enjoy the creativity of building a structure. The competitive element is usually subordinate to this creative process – though each group would like theirs to be the winning entry. Teams develop surprisingly strong loyalties to their product and defend not only its beauty but even its size or stability when these are plainly inferior to other models.

It is interesting to note the *proportions* of the finished artworks. Are there significantly more straws than bricks, for example? If so, how does player A, who supplied the bricks, feel about the imbalance? What kind of behaviour did player B use to ensure that straws were dominant in the construction? You might also want to look at leadership behaviour: did an authoritarian leader emerge in one group, for example? If so, did that team's product differ significantly in size or variety from the others?

Players of COLLABORATIVE ADVERSARY are effectively debriefed in terms of this particular view of industrial relations as a process of collaboration between workers and employers – though not necessarily always an equal collaboration. This is why it is important to play the game as one of a group of three exercises as described here, each designed to offer a different perspective on the basically uneasy alliance between capital and labour in organizational life.

SILVERWOOD: An example of industrial democracy

This represents Myers's (1978) third model. It appears idealistic at first glance because it is not based on the perpetuation of a two-class system, as is the collaborative-adversary model, but on a set of assumptions about the need for an entrepreneurial spirit in business and industry. This model is of a system in which the people who are influenced by it understand and agree with its purposes; have an equal hand in developing it, know how to use it, and feel themselves in control of it; can influence its revision; and receive timely feedback from it.

The kind of game you need to illustrate this argument is one in which all participants are united in some common task that relates to an outside party, person or agency. Such a game parallels in real life the entrepreneurial organization in which management and staff combine, for example, to conquer new markets, or increase sales in existing markets.

The most effective game we have set up to illustrate principles of industrial-democracy negotiation became known to the participants as SILVERWOOD. The group had to plan a campaign to raise a particular sum of money – none of which could be contributed by any group member – to be donated to a chosen charity. Other criteria were that the stated amount be sufficiently large to pose a challenge and evoke real effort, but not so large as to be unrealistic.

The rules were announced and the campaign plan began on a Wednesday evening, as part of a study course (two evenings a week for three months) for a certificate in management training. There were 20 participants, all from different organizations. One hour was devoted to the project out of a total class time of two and a half hours. The plan was to raise $1000 for a local women's refuge (the sum and its destination were chosen by the participants). The campaign was that every participant would take personal responsibility for raising $50. Everybody agreed that to donate any part of the money themselves – or for their families to donate it – would be 'cheating'. It was agreed that the money should be raised exclusively from colleagues at work, and that nobody should be asked to contribute more than $5. Since everybody worked for large organizations, this undertaking was not as difficult as it might have been.

During the following evening, Thursday, another hour was devoted during class time to finalizing the campaign. One group member (he worked for a security firm) brought official-looking badges for completion by the collectors; also a polaroid camera. He took a photo of everybody which he mounted on their badges. Another participant brought a set of receipt books which she stamped with the name the group had devised for the campaign –

Silverwood (which was the name of the women's refuge). All materials were then issued to the participants. One group member was appointed treasurer.

The group met again officially the following Wednesday evening, though many members had been in touch with each other privately during the week to discuss aspects of the campaign. A total of $750 had been collected.

By the Thursday evening of the same week the treasurer reported receipts totalling $1307.34. There was some suggestion that the $307.34 'surplus' be spent on a group celebration, but the general feeling was that the whole amount should go to the refuge, and the treasurer wrote a cheque accordingly.

Participants couldn't stop talking about this negotiation exercise. They considered it to be the perfect example of what could be achieved by industrial democracy and it beame a sort of touchstone by which the whole of the course was evaluated. People would say of some activity: 'That was almost as good as SILVERWOOD': the highest praise they could accord.

Finally in this chapter about focus games of human relations and labour relations we would like to introduce a game under a heading all by itself. Technically, it is not a focus game as we have defined the phrase, but it serves to focus players' attention on some of the major negotiation problems in 'compulsive relations'.

Compulsive relations

The following is an educational game in a cross-cultural setting. We designed it for local educators and social workers in Papua New Guinea to illustrate some problems and solutions for domestic violence (wife-beating). We think it could be adapted quite easily for other cultures and other settings – for example in the UK, America or Australia – to demonstrate some positive and negative ways of negotiating the potential violence and other problems of living with an alcoholic family member. It is also suitable for negotiation in other cases of domestic violence, or problems of young people in trouble with the police, etc.

You will see that only the game leader or deputies need to be literate – which may be of critical importance in some contexts where you might want to play the game. It is important that the information on the playing cards (see below) is realistic. If you want to write a set of cards to play this game with a group whose special problems are not professionally familiar to you, seek advice from somebody more qualified.

MERI WANTAIM MAN

This is a pidgin English phrase which is more usually in the form *man wantaim meri* or *man na meri* (man and wife). The inversion is deliberate here, to indicate that women are the focus of this game, since domestic violence is suffered primarily by women.

Objectives:

- to increase awareness of the causes of domestic violence in local (PNG) culture;
- to demonstrate a range of options open to battered wives;
- to emphasize the relative effectiveness of various strategies for dealing with domestic violence.

Number of players: a minimum of three, up to a probable maximum of seven players. If there are larger numbers, some people may prefer to be observers; otherwise players will have to wait a long time for their turn.
Time: half to one hour, depending on the number of players.
Materials:

- One floor cloth of dark, durable, washable material, like a tarpaulin. It should be as large as possible (which may mean fastening together a number of smaller pieces) and preferably square, at least ten foot by ten foot.
- A can of washable white paint and a good thick paintbrush.
- A large straight piece of wood to act as a ruler. The floor cloth should be marked out like a game board with white paint in at least ten squares and preferably 50–100 squares. Each square should be numbered like a Snakes and Ladders board, with number 1 in the bottom left-hand corner, the numbers ascending in order horizontally from line to line. The final number will be in the top left-hand corner. The floor cloth is a portable 'playing board' which can be rolled up into a manageable size and transported wherever required.

- A pack of cards, postcard size. Each card contains a statement and an instruction for the players, as described below.
- A pair of playing dice.

The game: The floor cloth is spread out on the floor of a large room or on flat ground in the open air. The cards are placed face down more or less at random intervals on various squares (or the game director may wish to write cards for every square). The first card should be somewhere near the beginning (square number 3 or 4) and the last almost at the end.

Players take it in turns to throw the dice. When they throw a double they begin the game by standing on square 1 until their turn comes round to throw again.

As the players continue to take turns throwing the dice, they move along the board to stand on the number corresponding to their throw. If the relevant square contains a card they pick it up and give it to the game director, who reads it aloud so the observers can hear. The player moves up or down the floor cloth, or stays in position, depending on the instructions on the card. The first player to complete the journey across the floor cloth is the winner, but the other players can continue if they wish until all have finished.

The game director may want to start a discussion with the players and observers, asking how they felt about the hazards of the game and how these relate to real-life problems of domestic violence. The game director can draw attention to the fact that, in the game, some strategies are penalized, while some are rewarded more highly than others. Do these penalties and rewards bear relation to the results of similar actions in real life?

However, it may be that players, for a number of reasons, are reluctant to discuss the implications of MERI WANTAIM MAN – and discussion should not be forced upon them. You will find the game is sufficiently thought-provoking as it is.

Suggestions for wording of cards: the cards are not in any special order but no.1 should probably be towards the end of the floor cloth 'board'. Also, the number of squares that players are asked to go forwards or backwards will depend on the total number of squares on the cloth.

1. Your husband beat you today. You did nothing. This was a

mistake because he will feel free to beat you again. Go back to square 1.

2. Your husband beat you today. You ran to your neighbour. This was good because maybe your man will be ashamed. Go forward three squares.

3. You told your husband the children were upset when he hit you. They can't sleep and their school work is suffering. He was shocked and promised not to hit you again. This was a very good thing to do because the children's education is important to him. Go forward ten squares.

4. You told your husband's father he beat you. Father scolded him and he apologized. This was good because your husband respects his father and will listen to him. Go forward ten squares.

5. You complained to your parents about the beatings. You want to go back to live with them but they think they will have to refund the bride price. This is not so under the law but perhaps they don't know it, and in any case it may not be easy for them if you go back to live with them. Go back five squares.

6. Your husband beat you again. You hit him back and he hit you harder. Violence only leads to more violence. You will have to find some other way of defending yourself. Go back five squares.

7. Your husband beat you today. You told him if it happened again you would leave him. Good! You are learning to stand up for yourself. Go forward three squares.

8. You talk to the village big man. He tells your husband not to beat you so hard. This was not a good thing for you to do. The village big man probably beats his own wife. Stay where you are and miss one turn.

9. Your husband still beats you. You talk to the Women's Council. They say your parents won't have to refund the bride money if you leave him. Perhaps now you can stay with your parents for a while. Go forward ten squares.

10. Your husband keeps telephoning you at work and insulting the switchboard staff. Your boss says you will lose your job if this continues. You arrange with a friend on the switchboard to hang up every time your husband calls. This is only a short-term solution. You will have to find a long-term way to deal with him. Stay where you are.

Chapter 3
Roleplays

This chapter is about roleplays and improvisations, which latter are structured more tightly than games and less so than simulations. The great advantage of roleplay and improvisation as a learning method is its versatility. The same roleplay can be enacted over and over again with different participants, whose responses will be different each time and thus provide fresh examples of the points you want to make. The actors can experiment with interpretation, learn something new about themselves and observe the effects on others of changes in their own behaviour. Roleplays can be scripted as well as improvised and may be monologues or dialogues between several people. They may have quite elaborate settings, or none at all. The roles may be realistic or fantastic. The actors may play themselves or assume characters. The whole purpose of both roleplay and improvisation is to answer the question 'What would happen if I/other people behaved like this?'

The following is a collection of roleplays we have found particularly effective with multicultural groups whose members have been from as many as 14 nationalities including Indians, Thais, Chinese, Japanese, Americans, Australians and Britons. These roleplays can be performed as dialogues between characters A and B or as group activities in which A and B are each represented by a consortium of players. Alternatively character A only has to 'leave a message' for B, stating A's position, and B has to take it from there. You may want to record these roleplays on video and play them back for more in-depth study. If you do, the behaviour of the actors can be interpreted in more detail to help them – and any other observers – become more effective negotiators in real life.

We include specific suggestions for debriefing each roleplay but there are general guidelines that apply to them all. For example:

- All definitions of negotiation (see eg Morley and Stephenson 1977:23-4) agree that it is a process of joint decision-making. Therefore, effective negotiation involves more than just a conflict of opinion. The negotiators should concern themselves with the form their joint action should take – otherwise agreement is impossible. What kind of compromises do they work out between them?

- Though it is assumed that both parties would like to reach agreement, all negotiation involves mixed motives. What kind of evidence indicates the presence of a hidden agenda?

- Negotiation involves strategic decision-making – dictated by the existence of conflicts of interest between the negotiators. If interests are to be defended, attempts will be made to outwit (or at least to match in wit) the opponent. What examples do you look for, of these tactics and manoeuvres? To what extent are they moderated by the need for cooperation between the contestants?

- Negotiation involves talking about a relationship before doing anything about it. You will find that, at one extreme, talking may involve a thoroughgoing discussion-to-consensus; at the other it may simply involve a change of bids. Remember, when you allocate the following roles, that A should not know B's goals in advance and vice versa.

Guided roleplays

APPLIED METALS

Role A: you are looking for a job and have applied to two companies, Applied Metals and Steel Incorporated. You have been accepted at both places. The salary is much higher at Steel Inc but you have been told that Applied Metals has a very cooperative working atmosphere and that it regularly rewards workers' achievements. If Applied Metals can make at least a 10 per cent rise in the salary presently offered, you want to accept their position. Otherwise you must turn it down. You have called this company on the telephone and reached the person in charge of employment. This person is from a different culture to your own. Your goal is to negotiate a higher salary. You can accept the position if and only if the salary is raised at least 10 per cent. Otherwise you must refuse it.

Role B: you are the person in charge of employment at Applied Metals. Recently you received a job application from a person of a different cultural background to your own. The applicant seems ideal and you have offered this person a job at the usual beginning salary. Since the applicant is talented and highly qualified you are prepared to negotiate the salary upwards a bit if necessary – for example a wage increase of between 5 and 7 per cent seems reasonable to you. Even 8 or 9 percent is remotely possible but this would be your top limit. Although you cannot guarantee it, it is likely this person will receive a 15 per cent rise at the end of the first year of employment. Your secretary has just informed you this person is now on the telephone wishing to speak with you. Your goal is to hire this applicant if at all possible; to negotiate the salary upwards if necessary but not higher than 9 per cent of what is presently being offered.

Notes for debriefing

The most frequent pattern is that A praises Applied Metals, reports the good things heard about it, stresses a desire to work there but emphasizes that prior commitments make it essential the salary be at least 10 per cent higher. B's response tends to vary depending on how free the roletaker feels to vary the company policy of Applied Metals.

Other leverage factors include:

- the economic environment (for example B may argue that this is a time of economic recession, therefore A cannot expect a higher salary);
- the age of the applicant (for example A may choose to emphasize his or her length of experience; on the other hand B may assume this will be A's first job);
- general salary levels at Applied Metals (for example B may claim that a higher salary for A would set a precedent that the company cannot afford).

THE FOREIGN BODY

Role A: you are travelling in a foreign country. Today, while eating out in a fairly expensive restaurant, you found what looked like part of an insect in your soup. You pointed this out and complained about it to the waiter – who insisted it was a spice. You don't believe it and insist on speaking to the manager, who is coming to your table now. You are angry and intend to demand that no charge be made for the meal and to state that the incident will be reported to the Department of Health.

Role B: you are the manager of a very good restaurant. The prices of the food selections may seem high to some people but you believe the quality of food and service makes the cost extremely fair. Your restaurant has a very good reputation and attracts many foreigners, one of whom is in your restaurant now. The waiter has just served this person a plate of soup and there seems to be some complaint about it. The waiter asks you to speak with the foreigner. You are going to the table now. Your goal is to listen to the problem and correct any misunderstanding. Unless the customer's demands are unreasonable, you want to be sure the customer is satisfied.

Notes for debriefing

One point of this roleplay is to illustrate how culture-specific is the display of emotion in public. What kind of behaviour does the irate customer adopt? And what kind of response does the restaurateur make? What kind of relationship develops between them as they talk?

Remember that all negotiation is about some kind of joint action – one example would be that the restaurateur offers to serve another portion of soup without the offending spice and the customer then agrees to refrain from further complaint. If this happens, how is the agreement reached? Through threats? What kind of threat?

Remember also that all negotiation takes place in a climate of mixed motives. What hidden agenda does the customer appear to have written? One example is some kind of ethnic prejudice. For instance, 'all foreigners are dirty', therefore this foreign restaurant is very likely to have insects in the soup. You can spot the existence of a hidden agenda when its owner refuses to accept any explanation, however reasonable, that the 'insect' is really a herb or spice. On the other hand, there may really have been an insect in the soup!

What tactics and manoeuvres does each contestant use? To what extent is this conflict moderated by a need for cooperation? For example, how hungry is the diner? How anxious is the restaurateur not to be reported?

FORCED CHOICE

This roleplay virtually ensures that A will feel some resentment, yet be unable to display it openly; B is also put in a position where mixed feelings predominate.

Role A: you are a researcher at a research institute specializing in intercultural communication. You are supervising a temporary intern whose cultural background is different to your own. You must evaluate the work of this intern and make a decision whether or not to extend the internship. You have had long talks with the intern about many things, sometimes unrelated to work, in order better to understand the intern's attitudes to life in general.

On the whole you are favourably impressed but there is one aspect of this intern's personality that you feel needs to be modified – an over-eagerness to please. The intern is becoming known as a person afraid to say no to any request. You believe this must change if the intern is to develop as a scholarly researcher.

In order to force the intern to take a stand and express a definite position, this afternoon you called the intern into your office and asked to buy the two concert tickets which the intern bought several weeks ago. You asked the intern to consider your request and give you a decision later. The intern is now back in your office looking rather worried. Your goal is to be firm about buying the tickets until the intern is able to refuse to sell. Once the intern refuses, you intend to explain the situation from your perspective.

Role B: you are a temporary intern at a research institute specializing in intercultural communication. You have been working under the direction of a senior researcher whose cultural background is different to your own and who is the supervisor who will evaluate your work at the end of the year. A poor assessment will not only affect the extension of your current position but also your entire career. You have a problem, because this person, who is from another country, has several times taken advantage of the circumstances to make unreasonable requests – which have nothing to do with your work. You have accepted them all, but today this supervisor called you into the office and asked you to sell two concert tickets to him for their original price. It even seemed to be hinted that you should hand them over as a gift, yet there are no more available and you had to queue up for hours to buy them and have promised to take your spouse to the concert.

The supervisor asked you to think it over and get back to him. You are now going to give him your reply. Your goal is politely to refuse to give or sell your concert tickets to your supervisor.

LATE ARRIVAL

Role A: this is the second time this week you have been late for work. You were hoping no one would notice, but after you arrived at your office, a written message came from your supervisor asking for an official explanation - which is to be placed in your personal file. This supervisor, whose cultural background is different to your own, is new and is obviously trying to do an effective job. You do not know him/her personally but wish this had been handled in an unofficial way.

You are almost never late for anything. This week, however, you have house guests from out of town and have been showing them around every evening after work. You have not been getting to bed until the small hours and this was the second morning you overslept. Fortunately, today is Friday and your guests are leaving this weekend. Next week things should be back to normal. You have decided to speak to your supervisor personally. Your goal is to apologize, explain the situation and request that the matter should not be officially recorded in your file.

Role B: you are a new supervisor in your office. This morning, one of your workers, who is from a culture different to yours, arrived late for work for the second time this week. This person's record appears to be good but this behaviour is not something you can allow to continue. You immediately sent this person a written message asking for an official explanation which would be included along with your report in their personal file. The worker is now outside your office requesting to speak with you.

Your goal is to be firm. Insist that the explanation be in writing and that it be completed before the end of this working day. Make it clear that if this behaviour continues, the worker's job will be at risk.

Before we describe the next game, a few words about videotaping roleplays. If you are working in international settings – such as an international conference – you can use participants as resource material for future occasions by video-recording some of their activities and obtaining their permission to play them with other groups.

This is not such a good idea when you are working in smaller social or professional circles. In these circumstances it is more diplomatic to replay the tape only to the actors and observers concerned in the making of it.

The following roleplays are not difficult to video with a fixed camera and the replays always evoke plenty of discussion. We suggest you treat each roleplay as an improvisation. Divide the group into teams of actors, with as many people in each team as there are parts in the roleplay, which you allocate to them. Give each team of actors an outline of their respective scenarios, making clear what kind of situation they are expected to create; then let them use their own creativity. Send them all off somewhere to rehearse their respective roleplays. They reconvene after an agreed interval, act out their scenes to each other and discuss the implications – and the videos serve as an additional resource.

THE SUPERMARKET

Bring a few supermarket items to the classroom, like packets of cereal, cans of fish etc – and a bottle of wine. Also, bring a copy of a Sunday edition of a British newspaper. If you're not directing this roleplay in the UK you may use anything visual that will identify the time and place of the roleplay as somewhere in the UK on a Sunday. Conduct the following rehearsal before you video.

Line participants up in front of a table, clutching their purchases as if they were waiting to pay at a checkout, with one person prominently holding the newspaper. Have somebody stand behind the table to take their money (this behaviour can be realistic or mimed, it doesn't matter).

Ask the shopper with the bottle of wine to step out of line (and out of camera shot) for a few seconds, as if to pick up some last-minute purchase from the shelves. Instruct the rest of the line to move up to close the gap, so that when the absentee returns s/he will have to push back in – an action which should be visibly resented by the other shoppers.

This shopper is now next in line to pay. The cashier looks at the bottle of wine and says: 'No, no! Seven o'clock!' several times; and refuses to accept money for the wine.

The shopper replies: 'But it's only 4 o'clock!' and again offers the money, which is again refused. The rest of the shoppers shuffle and mutter resentfully.

The person behind this shopper now says in an angry tone: 'Don't you know you're not allowed to buy alcohol on Sunday before 7 pm?'

Rehearse this scene a couple of times until it looks OK on the monitor, then record it.

Discussion questions when viewing the tape or recalling the scene include:

1. What happened during the scene? The following sequence seems to have occurred:

A - The shopper behaved in a socially unacceptable way by stepping out of the line and then trying to push back in, instead of returning to the tail of the queue. In the UK, queuing is taken very seriously and this behaviour was resented.

B - The shopper was then confronted by a non-native English-speaking cashier who could not explain fully that the shopper's proposed purchase of the wine could not be made legally before 7 pm on a Sunday.

C - This language barrier caused a complete communication breakdown, with shopper and cashier at cross purposes and the line at a standstill.

D - Because the shopper had become unpopular with the other people in the queue, they were not prepared to come to the rescue except in a critical way and this hostility even further confused the shopper.

2. How could the shopper have avoided all this embarrassment? One answer is by acquiring more information about archaic British legislation governing the sale of alcohol; but this isn't a very good answer, because nobody can learn everything there is to know about another culture. Also, such knowledge still might not have helped her when confronted, as one often is in the UK, with a cashier whose English is not fluent. A better answer might be that the shopper should become more sensitive to social nuances. For instance, a few moments' observation would probably have told her that people don't move in and out of queues. Thus she might have avoided antagonizing her fellow shoppers, so that when her misunderstanding arose with the cashier they would have been more happy to assist her.

You will find this roleplay creates much animated discussion among non-British players who have had any experience of supermarket shopping in the UK.

CORPORAL PUNISHMENT

The scene: two teachers stand with the school principal between them, three-quarters facing the camera, each with two or three students in line in front of them. Each teacher has a cane and strikes each student in turn on the extended palm. The students from the line nearer the camera turn towards the camera as they leave the teacher, and appear to be crying. One teacher seems to be quite pragmatic about hitting the students, the other teacher is more hesitant and strikes very lightly. The principal intervenes, saying: 'Hit harder! Hit harder! Make him learn his lesson – spare the rod and spoil the child!' The teacher tries to obey, but finally throws down the cane and runs away in tears.

Discussion: as with SUPERMARKET, you need to ask what happened and why it happened. And in this roleplay you need to know specifically:

- Would more information about the situation have helped the teacher who was distressed by the task of beating a student?
- Would more understanding of the cultural implications of the situation have helped this teacher?
- Or would nothing have been enough to prevent a values clash?

CORPORAL PUNISHMENT represents a real-life dilemma faced by many western teachers when they spend time working in other countries, particularly in Asia where corporal punishment of students is regarded very differently, compared, say, with American or British views of the subject.

DOG'S DINNER

This is a frankly theatrical roleplay which requires an area to be set aside as a stage with the audience seated in front. You need four volunteers with some experience of amateur dramatics or with innate acting abilities, or at least an extrovert temperament.

The scene: the four actors play two couples, hosts and guests respectively. The guests come to the door and are welcomed by the hosts. The hostess is carrying a small dog (a real dog for maximum effect, otherwise a toy), which is petted and admired by the guests. The hostess then excuses herself and goes offstage with the dog while the host takes the guests off in another direction, indicating he is leading the way to the dining room. Both couples return onstage, the guests praising the meal. One of them makes a joke about no dinner left over for the dog. Hosts look very embarrassed and change the subject. Guests suddenly gasp in horror and put their hands to their mouths.

When the roleplay is over, ask the audience:

- What happened?
- What was the roleplay about?
- Why were the hosts so embarrassed and the guests so horrifed? (Because the dog was the dinner!)
- How might the guests have handled the situation differently?
- Would more information about the local culture have helped them?
- Or a better understanding of the culture?
- How might they consider their options in such a fundamental cultural clash?

HOMEWORK

Set this up as for DOG'S DINNER.

The scene: two men and one woman, working late in the office. The woman should say something to indicate she is British or British-educated; one of the men – Bill – is also British.

The woman says she's tired and will go home, but still has work to do, so will get up early in the morning. Before leaving she asks Bill, who apparently lives nearby, if he would 'like to knock me up at 8 am?'

Bill takes this quite calmly, notes it in his diary, then makes an exclamation of impatience and says: 'Oh, how stupid!' Then he adds, to the other man, 'I say, old boy, have you got a rubber I could borrow?'

The other man says angrily, in an American accent: 'I think you're both disgusting!'

The woman and Bill look at each other in astonishment and reply: 'What on earth do you mean?'

HOMEWORK is particularly effective when some participants are American and some British, since the phrase 'knock me up' and the word 'rubber' carry sexual connotations for Americans but not for the British. In any cross-national setting it can be used to demonstrate the pitfalls of colloquialism.

Improvisations

Improvisations are more elaborate than the preceding guided roleplays and thus provide a transition between them and the more complex simulations.

DEVIL'S ADVOCATE

This is an improvisation about 'bottom lines' in negotiation. Writers on negotiation theory (see for example Fowler 1986, Kennedy, Benson and MacMillan 1980) argue the need for negotiating parties to identify levels of settlement rather than adopting a hard 'bottom line' as far as concessions are concerned. Kennedy, Benson and Macmillan (1980) describe three levels of settlement (L-I-M): 'L' is what the negotiator would like to achieve in ideal circumstances; 'I' is the intention to achieve something, even if the ideal is unattainable; and 'M' is what must be obtained as an absolute minimum. Fisher and Ury (1988) argue that the costs outweigh the benefits of adopting a hard bottom line and suggest instead that negotiators should develop a 'BATNA' – a best alternative to a negotiated agreement.

Objectives:

- to open players' ears, metaphorically, to arguments different to their own on a particular topic;

- to stimulate their imagination by perception of other viewpoints;
- to encourage them to be willing to change their minds if the evidence seems to warrant this;
- to increase players' flexible thinking: to enhance their ability to switch from one argument to another if the going gets tough.

Time required: about an hour.
Number of players: from about five people upwards.
Materials: there are preparations to make if you want to play DEVIL'S ADVOCATE. You will have to search through newspapers and journals to find articles that discuss topics such as the following:

- equal employment opportunities and affirmative action;
- the power of trade unions;
- government interventions in business and industry;
- the special problems faced by women in management;
- immigrant labour;
- personnel information systems versus employees' right to privacy;
- employee sabotage and theft;
- substance abuse by employees;
- and so on.

No doubt you will be able to think of other controversial problems that employers face in today's climate of industrial, social, political, economic and technological change. You will find the following journals are useful:

- *Harvard Business Review;*
- *Industrial Relations Journal;*
- *Personnel;*
- *Personnel Journal;*
- *Personnel Management;*
- *Training and Development Journal.*

Some of these journals are British, some American, but they are all sold internationally. Any good business library will stock them and more like them. Make multiple copies of articles that strike you as controversial or at least express a definite viewpoint.

Roles and rules: assemble players in small groups of five to seven people. Identify a leader in each group who is willing to act also as a reporter. Call all group leaders to you and give each one copies of the articles you have collected (which you will have edited judiciously if they were lengthy). If there are five people in a group, give the leader copies of four articles, one for each team member, on subjects as varied as possible (the leader won't need a copy). Thus, for example, one group of five team members may receive copies of four articles respectively about administrative problems in organizations due to employees taking long maternity or paternity leave; employees being forced to accept redundancy packages or early retirement due to organizational downsizing without consultation with worker representatives; the stress on employees of having to relocate due to an organizational policy of decentralization; whether employees should be allowed to smoke anywhere in their workplace. (Note that all groups can have copies of the same set of articles.)

Go briefly through these articles with group leaders; get them to identify the topic or theme of each article. Ask them to do the following after returning to their respective groups:

- allocate one of these topics to each team member at random (without giving them the relevant article);
- ask each player in turn to talk to the group for about three minutes about their allotted topic, expressing their personal opinion and their feelings about it;
- time each speaker and stop them after three to five minutes;
- when all have spoken their minds, give each speaker the relevant article and allow them time to read it (about five minutes): the objective is to give them further viewpoints and insights to the topic;
- then ask each group member in turn to speak for another three to five minutes, arguing with as much conviction as possible a point of view opposite to their own previously expressed positions;
- initiate a short discussion and take notes, about how group members perceived their dual roles.

Notes for discussion

Your job is to monitor the groups (if more than one) so they all keep more or less to the same time schedule; then to reconvene all groups in plenary session in which group leaders compare notes and team members add any further comments that occur to them. Discuss with everybody the costs of adopting too 'hard' a stance on any topic, including the danger of losing face if one's arguments are countered by other evidence. Link this idea to the disadvantages of adopting a rigid bottom line in negotiation.

PLAYBACK

This improvisation was designed for an organizational client with a strong corporate culture whose managers wanted to learn how to negotiate with companies of very different orientation. We include it here to illustrate how important it is for people to create their own negotiation style – one with which the team feels comfortable – even if it is an unusual style, perhaps unique. Negotiators can put themselves in a false position if they try to bargain on territory that belongs to the other side; though often it appears to them that they have no choice but to do so. It's much smarter to move your opponent on to your ground and argue from there.

For example, if you want to coax a personal loan out of a reluctant bank manager you may be tempted to use financial arguments that are, however, much more familiar to the bank manager than to you. You put yourself at a disadvantage. Whereas if you concentrate on the soundness of your reasons for wanting the loan (about which you know a lot more than the bank manager) you are more likely to win your case.

The client for whom we designed PLAYBACK is a theatre company in the north of England whose government subsidy at that time had been cut so drastically that its members were faced with the need to attract funding from the local private sector – but didn't know how to negotiate it, which is why they called us in. Our problem was to find them a strategy which they could pursue with conviction, since none of them was businesslike in the profit-and-loss sense of the phrase.

The company consisted of a director/manager, assistant manager, secretary, publicity officer, a woman responsible for costumes and properties, a small team of stagehands and technicians, and a cast of actors. They were a close-knit group of mutually supportive people, feelings-oriented rather than pragmatic: not one of them had any formal business training. Thus the corporate personality of our client was a critical factor in our consultant-client relationship.

When we got to know everybody in this little theatre - and discussed its policies and productions with the regional arts association - we were convinced it had a great deal to offer the local community. We also felt the enterprise had something to offer the business world, yet its members had no experience of the persuasive techniques needed to influence hard-nosed business people to support it.

Eventually we designed a simulation in which they could let their artistic imagination run riot - in the hope that the resulting creative energy would produce some useable strategy. We matched game setting and role descriptions to the drama-trained personalities of the players. If you disapprove of it, yet would like to use the improvisation, you can always change it to that of any small business offering a more conventional service to the public.

Time required: PLAYBACK takes about an hour to play, and you should allow at least another hour for players to talk about it afterwards.

Number of players: when we first played the game there were 14 participants. We have discovered since that it can be played with a minimum of six to virtually any number. If there are only six players you will be able to form only one team of three, with one observer and two representatives of the business community.

Materials: the only materials you need are an audio cassette player/recorder, microphone and tape for each 'production team' (of three to five members) and a neutral observer for each team. You will also need a room large and uncluttered enough to move about in comfortably. We were able to use the smaller of the two theatre spaces, which was ideal.

If you have facilities and time, players can create a video instead of an audio recording. However, this requires a camera for each playing group.

Setting and roles: we gave each team a cassette player and a copy of the following instructions to each team member:

Team Members, you and your colleagues are the 'Madam', hosts and hostesses of a brothel in a building owned by the local authority of a small South American town called Sueno. Until the present time your landlords have taken a relaxed attitude towards your trading practices – in fact several of them have been your satisfied customers for years. Unfortunately, a puritanical mayor was elected recently who persuaded the council to raise your rent ten times in an effort to bankrupt you. You cannot increase custom without everybody becoming exhausted, therefore you need to attract private funding if you are to stay in business. And for that you need publicity. There is no television in Sueno and no newspaper, so you have decided to advertise for sponsorship through the local radio channel – though you will have to word your appeal tactfully so as not to offend the susceptibilities of this small Catholic community.

Your task is to write and record a 1 – 3 minute radio appeal. You have half an hour to plan, rehearse and record it. Then it will be played to representatives of Sueno's business community who will decide whether your argument has been sufficiently persuasive for them to sponsor you.

The two observers were each given a copy of this scenario, with a request that they observe the decision-making processes of each team respectively. Two players remained, who were told they were 'representatives of Sueno's business community'. They were given a copy of the team members' instructions, and the following instructions:

Representatives of the business community: your task is to listen to two 'radio appeals' and decide which one you prefer and why. After hearing the appeals, please complete the following questionnaire and be prepared to discuss your answers with the group.

Commercial A:
Has no appeal for me/has some appeal/is very appealing

1 ....5 10

Is of poor sound quality/fairly good sound/very good sound

1 ....5 10

Lacks imagination/fairly imaginative/original and innovative

1 ....5 10

Commercial B:
Has no appeal for me/has some appeal/is very appealing

1 ....5 10

Is of poor sound quality/fairly good sound/very good sound

1 ....5 10

Lacks imagination/fairly imaginative/original and innovative

1 ....5 10

Rules: we gave the theatre group about five minutes to read and absorb their instructions and ask any procedural questions (in fact they didn't ask anything though they laughed a lot). They were reminded they had half an hour to complete their recordings, under the eye of the observers – who would take notes but not otherwise be involved. The two representatives of the business community were sent off to have a cup of coffee with strict instructions to return in 20 minutes.

Action: the two teams were then asked to begin their task. One of the Madams called her brothel Fiesta and herself La Fiesta. Her tactics were to assume an authoritative leadership style and to identify relevant talents her staff might possess, while simultaneously encouraging them to use them.

She reminded her girls and boys that though they knew everything about the provision of their specialist services, they knew nothing about making radio commercials. They were all working people, she said. She herself was of humble origins, having worked her way up to her management position from the shop floor, literally. Did her boys and girls have any experience in writing, acting, voice production or stage directing?

She showed considerable skill in utilizing what she found, and in time-management (not surprisingly, since she was a theatre director in real life). One young lady said she had been a member of her school debating team. La Fiesta therefore auditioned her voice and that of one of the men, and asked both to write for three minutes on 'My best customer' so she could judge their literary skills. Meanwhile, she and the other two team members familiarized themselves with the sound-recording equipment.

The other team was equally busy. They called the brothel Mi Casa Su Casa and the Madam was Señor Felix. Like La Fiesta he took charge from the beginning, but his strategic plan was based on his confidence in himself as a presenter (he was an actor). Therefore he would broadcast the appeal in person.

He dispatched one of his ladies to ask us, as representatives of the radio station, whether he could make the broadcast 'live'. This was a tricky one, because such a tactic might well give his team a major advantage over the other. Would it be an 'unfair' advantage? After some thought (game directors need to be quick on their feet) we agreed to his suggestion, aware that we were taking a risk because the other team might resent our decision.

While this manoeuvre was in progress at Mi Casa Su Casa, La Fiesta's scriptwriter had written some draft copy which was read aloud by the girl with the chosen voice. La Fiesta asked the observer for constructive criticism, which was a coercive tactic to get him 'on-side' so he would report favourably on the game behaviour of the team. He warmly approved of the writer's idea for La Fiesta to accept advertising from local businesses, whose copy would be displayed at strategic points throughout the brothel. He offered helpful suggestions for the final draft of the copy, as did the team members. The 'voice' was then given short but intensive training by La Fiesta and also by the observer, who by this time had abandoned all attempt at impartiality.

Back at Mi Casa, Señor Felix sketched out his 'act', which included brief appearances by his three teammates.

We had warned the teams that after half an hour we would call in the business reps, whether or not they were ready. In fact, both were well prepared. Team leaders tossed a coin to see who would go first, and La Fiesta won.

The recording was of good quality and the girl with the golden voice sounded very seductive. Potential advertisers were reminded that their copy would be seen by a large number and a wide range of potential customers. They were offered a reasonable scale of rates, from a modest hand-written ad in the front hall to posters in the bedrooms and expensive ads on bedheads and ceilings.

Señor Felix read his appeal from behind a screen so he could be heard but not seen, which seemed a fair compromise. He asked the local business community to fund scholarships for the employees of Mi Casa, to enable them to take lessons in dancing and singing. He succeeded in hinting at all sorts of innuendos in words like 'entertainment' and 'exotic dancing'; and his 'girls' backed him by singing an adaption of a Beatles song: 'I do care so much for money, 'cos money can buy me love'.

Observation: the 'business representatives' listened to both appeals with enjoyment, completed their questionnaires and then discussed them, and the observers added their reports to balance the whole procedure. La Fiesta's was the winning team by a whisker.

We debriefed the whole exercise by drawing attention to the negotiating strengths we had seen in action: confident and effective leadership; close and supportive teamwork; lack of threatening or coercive behaviour but reliance instead on information-sharing, questioning and rewarding; imaginative and innovative strategies and tactics; competence in execution; time management, and so on. We suggested these were the strengths that should be harnessed to work on the business community.

The ending of the story is a happy one. The theatre company actually used both strategies that emerged from the game – they persuaded a large food manufacturer, which owned a local biscuit factory, to fund four scholarships each year to pay for young actors' salaries in productions at the theatre; and they conducted a successful marketing campaign to attract advertising in the theatre foyer, on progammes, etc. When we last heard from the company, the manager was planning to mount sponsors' commercials 'live' as curtain-raisers to some of the shows.

She was good enough to say that PLAYBACK had been a tremendous learning experience for her team, and astute enough to recognize that the most important result of that learning was to inspire every member of the company with the confidence that they could take on the business world and win.

GOING FINISH

This is an improvisation about a different kind of negotiation: the negotiation of meaning between the reader and any written material – texts, documents, contracts, job descriptions,

91

memoranda, instruction manuals, journal articles, advertisements and so on.

GOING FINISH was designed for a class of local students studying a first-year business course as part of a business degree at the University of Papua New Guinea, Port Moresby. We cited it in Chapter 1 as an example of a simulation that could originally have been more appropriately designed with more knowledge of the culture. It is presented here in its final version. All the instructions were written originally for non-native and not very fluent English speakers. They can be rephrased if greater sophistication is required. Also, the number of advertisements can be increased and worded with more subtlety if your players have greater command of English.

Scenario: potential buyers negotiate with sellers over items advertised for sale but not open to inspection. Clues to the real nature of the goods (and therefore pointers to questions buyers should ask) are hidden in the wording of the advertisements.

The game title refers to a popular kind of advertisement in the Papua New Guinea (PNG) *Post Courier* whereby foreigners and transient businesspeople and academics try to dispose of property before they leave the country. The title can be changed to suit other local conditions and the 'for sale' advertisements in any local newspaper can be used as models. In our examples below, the prices of the goods for sale are given in the local currency. Obviously, you will reword them to include prices in pounds, dollars, yen, whatever.

Objectives:

- to practise critical appraisal of a written text;
- to improve skills of negotiation on the basis of a written document;
- to improve students' use of English (optional).

Time: about 2 hours, including discussion.

Number of players: minimum of two to any number.

The improvisation can be between two people (a buyer and a seller) or between two (or multiples of two) groups of people, one group consisting of sellers and the other of buyers. A buying group is made up of the following characters (who of course can be played by anybody):

- one or two parents;
- teenage son;
- teenage daughter;
- grandmother;
- grandfather.

The instructions below assume there is only one person playing the buyer.They are easily re-written if your participant numbers are large enough to form groups.

Materials:

- a table for each pair or group with some kind of screen between them so 'buyer(s)' and 'seller(s)' cannot see each other;
- an audio cassette recorder on each table, if you want to record the discussion for later analysis;
- for each player, one copy of:
- role instructions for buyers and sellers respectively (all buyer instructions are the same, and so are those for sellers);
- 'advertisement';
- 'facts not included in the advertisement';
- 'points for discussion' (you can give a copy of this to all participants after the game, unless you prefer to debrief only verbally).

Rules: organize players into pairs or two groups (at least) of about three to six people in each. Designate buyers and sellers. Give copies of instructions to all players as follows:

Give to all buyers: role instructions for buyers; and the advertisement(s). When the game is over, give each buyer a copy of facts not included in the advertisement(s).

Give to all sellers:

- role instructions for sellers;
- the advertisement(s);
- facts not included in the advertisement(s).

Give all players about ten minutes to read and discuss their respective information in private (groups can find another room, use the corridor, stairwell, etc, for greater privacy). Move about yourself from group to group to make sure everybody understands what the game is about and what they have to do. Then seat all players in pairs or paired groups at tables with a screen between them; and announce that bargaining can begin.

After about 20 minutes, or longer if people are enjoying themselves, call a halt and initiate a discussion.

The advertisements

GOING FINISH: FAMILY GOING THURSDAY. THESE ITEMS FOR URGENT SALE:

BICYCLE: English Raleigh boy's bicycle. Bodywork in beautiful condition. Colour racing green. Dropped handlebars. Mean machine for daring rider. Many extras (saddle-bag, toolkit, etc). Price 200K.

VIDEO CASSETTE PLAYER: Sanyo, stereo, terrific tone, great picture. You can watch your favourite movies over and over again. Comes with its own attractively designed TV and video table. Price 300K.

KITCHEN BLENDER: Sanyo, nearly new, complete set of four blades, two bowl sizes. Will chop, blend, etc, quicker than you would believe. Colour white, durable enamel finish, hardly a mark on it. Price 50K.

PARTY DRESS: lovely blue silk, calf-length, short sleeves, full skirt, average size, youthful style. You'll be the best dressed girl at the party. Perfect condition. Worn only once, looks like a Paris model. Price 100K.

Facts not included in the advertisement

Bicycle: as in ad, but:

- no gears;
- badly worn tyres;
- no pump;
- small wheels, suitable for a small rider only.

VCR: as in ad, but plays only, won't record programmes from TV.
BLENDER: as in ad, but juicer attachment is missing.
DRESS: 'average size' refers to American or British standards. Its measurements are to fit a woman of bust size 36″, waist 24″, hips 38″.

Instructions to sellers

In this game we are pretending that you have put a 'Going Finish' advertisement in the PNG *Post Courier*. It is a larger ad than usual because you want to make the goods sound attractive to sell them more quickly.

A family a long way away wants to buy the whole lot but they are not able to come and see the goods. Instead, they will talk to you on the telephone.

Your religion does not allow you to put any lies in the advertisement, but you do not have to tell the whole truth.

During the telephone conversation you are not allowed to tell any lies, but you may answer any question by saying 'I don't know'.

Instructions for buyers

In this game we are pretending you saw a 'Going Finish' advertisement in the PNG *Post Courier*.

You would like to buy all the items but you are not able to travel to see the goods. You will talk to the sellers on the telephone.

You know the sellers' religion will not allow them to write or tell any lies, but that does not mean they have to write or tell the whole truth.

These are the reasons you are interested in the advertisement:

- your father, mother, teenage son and teenage daughter all live with you;
- your son is now nearly 6 ft tall;
- his old bicycle is now much too small for him and you want to buy him another;
- he wants a racing bicycle in good condition;
- he cannot afford repairs, tools or replacements;
- your father wants a VCR (video) to record his favourite TV shows;
- your mother wants a kitchen blender to squeeze fresh fruit;
- your daughter wants a party dress. Her measurements are: bust 22"; waist 18"; hips 34".

Points for discussion

You should be able to judge a piece of writing by:

1. The *facts* it contains.
2. The *opinions* it expresses.
3. What it *leaves out*.

4. The *hidden meaning*.
5. The *background* of the writer. Where does the writer seem to be 'coming from'?

1. Were there enough *facts* in the advertisement to describe the goods accurately? As you will see, the answer is no.
2. The *opinions* expressed in the advertisement.

Phrases like 'beautiful condition' and 'mean machine' are merely expressions of the writer's opinion and can be misleading. Nearly half the paragraph about the VCR is opinion, not fact.

3. What did the advertisements *leave out*? Important information was missing from the advertisement, for example:

- On behalf of your son, did you ask about the condition of the bicycle tyres, the size of the bicycle, whether it had a pump and gears?
- On behalf of your daughter, did you ask about the measurements of the dress?
- On behalf of your father, did you ask whether the video cassette player was also a video recorder?
- On behalf of your mother, did you ask whether the blender had a juicer, since this was very important to her?

4. *Hidden meanings* in the advertisement. You can argue that all advertisements have hidden meanings. They are intended to persuade you to buy the goods whether you want them or not, and to make you want something you would probably never have thought of by yourself. Therefore you need to check advertisements out very carefully.

5. The *background* of the writer. In this case you know the writer of the advertisement wants to get rid of the goods as quickly as possible because he has advertised in the 'Going Finish' section of the paper. Therefore you can't afford to take anything on trust.

Whenever you read anything, think about the person who wrote it. Judging by what they wrote, what kind of person do you think they are? What do they really want you to believe?

RELOCATION

This is an improvisation designed to study collective bargaining as a dimension of industrial relations. It also illustrates some of the pitfalls of sequential bargaining: that is, of adopting in advance a series of fixed positions rather than listening with an open mind to what the other party has to say.

Time required: about two hours; longer if the group is large or if you want to expand the scenario. The negotiation can run for a whole day or even longer.

Number of players: this improvisation works best with a fairly large group, say of 12 people upwards, but you can play it with any number above seven; or you can arrange a larger group into independent sub-groups of about seven people, and compare notes afterwards.

Materials: Normal classroom facilities including lots of flip-chart paper and big felt-tipped pens in various colours for players to make posters with, if they want to.

Scenario and roles: explain that players will take the respective roles of:

- chairman of the board;
- managers;
- employees who are to be relocated;
- employees who are not to be relocated;
- union representative(s). If there is more than one, one will be the elected shop steward.

They are all part of an organization which is an office-equipment distributor. The organization plans to relocate a section of its stores department closer to the point where repairs and servicing are undertaken by mechanics. However, the stores' employees have worked together in the same location for many years, have developed into a close workgroup and are members of the same union.

Roles and rules: explain that players will have about half an hour (or more) to read their roles (see below), discuss their strategies with teammates and lobby the other side informally. Then announce that collective bargaining will begin.

On one side of the table will be the chairman and managers; on the other at least one employee to be relocated and one who will not; and a union representative.

When we directed RELOCATION with a group of business students the 'employers' jumped at an opportunity (when the woman playing a very authoritarian and reactionary shop steward left the room for a few moments) to consult personally with the 'employees'. They poured them coffee, argued the merits of the proposed relocation and won their support by offering transportation allowances. The result was that, on her return, the shop steward found her authority eroded. She tried to call a strike but the workers flatly refused to accept her decision. They agreed to the relocation in spite of her passionate protests that it was not in their long-term interests to do so – a factor that had emerged clearly during the game.

Another time, a group of workers put up posters all round the room, demanding strike action if the relocation went ahead. This made the shop steward's position at the negotiating table very difficult, since he personally disapproved of strikes and was prepared to negotiate tirelessly for compromise.

Notes for discussion

When playing RELOCATION, the objectives of the 'employers' may be to effect the relocation while maximizing industrial peace (that is, as much as possible to prevent workers losing productivity during the period of relocation), to discover the real sources of their likely resistance before entering into actual negotiation, and so on. The workers' objectives may be to reject the relocation altogether, or to seek to have it modified in some way. In other words, the game elicits various forms of bargaining behaviour.

How might the negotiators have found more successful ways and means of achieving their objectives? How might they have recognized and discarded tactics that were unlikely to be effective, and developed more promising ones?

Rolecards

Chairperson and managers: you have decided upon a series of tactics which is sequential. You will begin by trying to arrange a consultation with the employees as a group, without their shop steward(s). If this tactic fails, you plan to read aloud a written directive signed by the managing director, explaining the reasons for the relocation and the advantages to the employees and the company. If the union representative(s) continue to resist reloca-tion, you plan to threaten to issue dismissal notices. In the last resort you are prepared to forget the whole idea of relocation. The chairman will make the final decision.

Union representative(s): you have decided on a series of tactics which is sequential. You begin by trying to arrange a private consultation with the chairman of the board, knowing that s/he will make the final decision about the proposed relocation. If this tactic fails, you plan to issue a written directive signed by yourself as shop steward, explaining the employees' objections to the relocation and the advantages to the company of them staying where they are. If management continues to insist on the relocation, you plan to threaten a series of strikes. In the last resort you are prepared to advise your members to accept the relocation.

Employees to be relocated under the proposed scheme: you are deeply concerned about this proposed relocation. It will involve you in lengthy commuting – which means less time at home with your families – and separation from colleagues with whom you have worked closely and comfortably for years. Your shop steward tells you s/he has decided on a series of tactics, all of which you approve:

- to negotiate with the chairman and senior management to reconsider their decision to relocate;
- to issue a written statement of your objections to the relocation and the advantages to the company of staying where you are.
- to threaten strike action if necessary.

Employees who are not at present affected by the proposed relocation: you are not personally concerned with this proposed relocation because it doesn't affect you, though you will be sorry to lose colleagues who are also friends, and sympathize with the problems they will face over relocation. You support industrial action by your shop steward on these employees' behalf, but your support stops a long way short of a strike.

THE RBO GAME

Douglas McGregor, in his famous book. *The Human Side of Enterprise* (1960) argues that people's behaviour reflects their values or attitudes towards other people. One type of attitude,

which he describes as being based on a 'Theory X', comprises a set
of expectations that:

- people inherently dislike work and will avoid it if they can;
- most people tend to avoid responsibility, have relatively little
  ambition, prefer security above all and need to be told what to
  do;
- therefore most people in the workforce must be directed,
  manipulated, coerced, rewarded, threatened and punished in
  order to get them to work to achieve organizational goals.

On the other hand, argues McGregor, there is another set of
assumptions – a 'Theory Y':

- that work comes as naturally to most people as rest and play;
- that most people are willing to exercise self-direction and self-
  control in the service of objectives to which they feel personally
  committed;
- that most people, under appropriate conditions, will not only
  accept but actively seek responsibility;
- that most people are capable of a high degree of imagination,
  ingenuity and creativity in the solution of organizational
  problems in which they have a genuine interest;
- that the intellectual capacities of most people in the workforce
  are underestimated and underused;
- that development of employees' potential and their commitment to objectives will occur as a function of the rewards
  associated with this development in a kind of self-fulfilling
  prophecy.

McGregor's Theories X and Y have important implications for
negotiation training. For example, many union leaders don't
believe that managements want to work in harmony with them, or
are capable of being rational and open-minded about industrial
relations; and most managers appear to feel just as negative
towards workers and their representatives. In other words, both
parties assume that Theory X holds good for their relationship.

The following improvisation is an attempt to demonstrate that
adoption by both sides of Theory Y is likely to be more productive
in negotiation: but THE RBO GAME – so-called for reasons that will

become apparent – also has another purpose: to counter criticism of gaming activities of this kind.

In the introduction to this book we referred to criticism of games and simulations for being less than effective negotiation exercises. Morley and Stephenson (1977:53) for example draw attention to the fact that many aspects of negotiation behaviour are not reproduced at all in roleplaying debates; and of those that are, nobody seems to know for sure which are well reproduced and which are not.

In particular, according to Morley and Stephenson, we do not know to what extent participants respond interpersonally to negotiation simulations rather than as representatives of groups engaged in collective bargaining. THE RBO GAME was designed to emphasize this collective-bargaining aspect of negotiation, and is based on two concepts. One is that of 'relationship by objectives' (RBO), an intervention process introduced in 1975 by the US Federal Mediation and Conciliation Service (see, for example, Myers 1978:79–81). The second concept is the use of RBO methods for experimental research in collective bargaining, first suggested (as far as we know) by J E McGrath in 1966. McGrath's paradigm requires that bargaining simulations should fulfil four needs:

- participants should in real life be parties to the negotiation that is the subject of the simulation;
- the simulation task should be one of discussion;
- the issues under discussion should be realistic, important to the parties and sufficiently complex for genuine debate;
- there should be a real-life conflict of interest between the parties, independent of the simulated scenario.

THE RBO GAME requires you, as game leader, to create a scenario with which the players can directly identify. Therefore, it is suitable for inclusion with in-house training programmes in fairly large organizations where management training, dispute resolution, conflict negotiation and so on are regularly practised. We have played it successfully for the training department of a nationwide brewery with a turbulent history of industrial relations, and a government service department which was under heavy criticism from its clients.

THE RBO GAME is in two parts.

The RBO Game: the video

You need a video that lasts about 20 minutes and depicts a contract negotiation in which poor attitudes on the shop floor spill over into the negotiations. You can probably find something appropriate from your local supplier of training videos. However, if you can get together with the industrial relations officer and training staff you can design your own scenario and make a video that will not only provide the basis for Part 2 of THE RBO GAME but will serve also as a learning process and tool for the staff. The scenario should have the following components:

- a confrontation between a supervisor and a shop steward;
- a number of problems in company–union relations that emerge during the confrontation and form a background to it;
- a bargaining session between management and union, based on the confrontation.

It is not as difficult as you might think to write a script in two scenes, based on the above, then to coach four 'actors' (two for each scene) and video the whole thing. Even if you are not an experienced camera operator, or do not have access to such a person, you can set up a fixed camera and seat each pair of actors at a table very close to each other and half-face to the camera. If you have to do this (though such an arrangement is less than ideal), write out the actors' lines on 'idiot sheets' and post the sheets on easels behind each actor but out of camera range, so the actors will appear to be looking at each other while in fact reading their scripts. End the lines on each sheet at a natural break (not in the middle of a sentence or argument); then you can stop the camera when you need to change the sheets. On the other hand you can coach the actors in improvisation.

Whichever way you do it, you will find with practice that you all become quite adept at this makeshift exercise: the results, though they may not be of top professional standard, may pleasantly surprise you. There is no denying, however, that a more effective arrangement is to have a camera operator.

The first scene is between a supervisor and a shop steward. It should last about ten minutes and describe the confrontation. For example, the supervisor may announce a higher production target and the shop steward may respond with a demand for increased pay for the affected workers. During the discussion other and more longstanding grievances will be referred to: and here we emphasize that any such grievances should be 'real', in the sense that the client organization is actually experiencing them. The second scene (also of about ten minutes) depicts a negotiation between a senior manager and a union leader over a new contract.

You will find it helpful to write an outline for all participants in the dispute before you begin to write the actual dialogue. The outline could usefully include a bargaining range for scene 2, showing possible settlement points and the corresponding costs to the company for the period of the contract. The following example is of a dispute over penalty rates for workers on night shift which escalates into a demand by the union for a higher overtime rate. The example below of a bargaining range for the negotiation in scene 2 is adapted from Morley and Stephenson (1977:52).

Suggested outline for dialogue: Scene 1
1. Some reference to a history of bad relations between supervisor and shop steward over production figures on the night shift.
2. Explicit reference to an existing contract: an extra 50 pence per hour is paid for nightwork.
3. Confrontation between supervisor and shop steward when supervisor tries to impose a higher production quota for nightwork; shop steward insists on a higher overtime rate in compensation.
4. The matter is referred to senior management for negotiation with the union.

Suggested outline for dialogue: Scene 2
1. Union demand: a 50 pence per hour increase to £1.00 per hour.
2. Management position: rejection of the demand.
Bargaining range:

	0	10	20	30	40	50	
Company	——————	——————	——————	——————	——————	——————	Union
Total	1000	2000	3000	4000	5000	6000	

The top line represents the proposed increase, from zero to the full 50p, with the company position at one end and that of the union at the other. The bottom line represents the cost to the company over, say, a one-year contract under the present arrangement and what increase they would face at the various bargaining positions.

Once you've got this outline, you can write the dialogue for the actors, or coach them in an improvisation. You should end the negotiation in deadlock because for the purposes of the simulation each party is treating the other as an adversary and both are working on 'Theory X' principles.

Having acquired the necessary video, you are now ready to play THE RBO GAME; and you, the industrial relations people and the personnel department will already have benefited from the experience of making the video.

THE RBO GAME

This simulation is between participants who in real life are representatives of labour and management respectively. The objectives of the game are for both parties:

- to identify the problems in their relationship and relate these to Theory X assumptions about the nature of the relationship;
- to clarify their expectations of the relationship;
- to develop the means to solve their problems by assuming Theory Y principles.

Time required: one day.

Number and characteristics of participants: they will be real-life union representatives or members; and supervisors or middle managers. The simulation requires a minimum of two teams, each with a mediator.

Materials:

- the video as described above;
- a blank sheet of ruled paper for each participant, headed: 'What do you expect to gain from this programme?'
- an outline of the major differences between Theory X and Theory Y assumptions.

Roles and rules: divide participants into at least two teams of negotiators – one representing labour, the other management – and a mediator.

Explain the objectives of the simulation, then pass round copies of the questionnaire asking participants to respond to the question: 'What do you expect to gain from this programme?'

Collect their replies, issue them with the 'Theory X and Theory Y' handout, then show them the video. Ask the teams to do the following:

- analyse the attitudes of the supervisor and the shop steward in the video they have just seen;
- list the problems in the company–union relationship as illustrated or implied in the video;
- identify any behaviour or attitudes that seemed to be based on Theory X assumptions;
- recommend strategies for changing this behaviour to conform more to Theory Y assumptions.

After this team exercise, all teams reassemble to discuss their reports. Up to this point, the process should have been an exercise in group dynamics, an attempt to stimulate participants' thinking and an important psychological groundwork to the programme itself.

Phase 1

Now separate the group into labour and management components. In their separate conferences, ask participants to respond to these questions:

- What should the other party be doing to improve labour–management relations?
- What should you be doing?

Collect the responses and with the help of the mediators collate all similar answers. Restate negative complaints as positive goals. Then ask the mediators to draw up four lists, based on:

1. According to the company, the union should . . . . .
2. According to the company, the company should . . . .
3. According to the union, the company should . . . . .
4. According to the union, the union should . . . .

This ends Phase 1 of the simulation.

Phase 2

Now labour and management meet together to review the four lists to narrow the selection of mutually agreeable objectives. You will find almost all goals touch on:

- labour–management communications;
- management attitudes and practices;
- union attitudes and practices;
- training and human resources development.

Phase 3

Ask the entire group to consolidate the lists into a single list of mutual objectives. Get them to break this down into four parts, with each part assigned to one of the original teams for study.

The original teams then reconvene. They must develop action steps to accomplish the objectives.

Now reassemble management and union groups in separate conferences to review the team proposals and to formulate specific action steps for achieving the objectives on which the two sides have already agreed.

Phase 4

The entire group reassembles to hammer out differences.

Phase 5

A review of the goals, action steps and assignments of responsibility is made and a timetable for resolution of the problems is adopted.

As a final comment, we emphasize that although THE RBO GAME seems extremely complicated when you first read it, it becomes much less so after the first playing, and in any case is well worth the effort if you have sufficient time to play and debrief it. Participants find it most rewarding and thought-provoking. The exercise provides real practice for them in negotiation skills as well as giving them insights to strategic planning.

Chapter 4
Simulations

TOWN AND GOWN

The inspiration for the following simulation was a showdown some years ago between members of a motorbike gang and police officers on Mount Panorama racetrack during an annual national bike race.

Mount Panorama is just outside the university town of Bathurst in rural New South Wales. Normally it is a pleasant, peaceful country town; but on two weekends a year it came dramatically to life with national car and bike races. Though the car race continues to be very popular, there have been no bike races since the events on which this game is very loosely based. We would like to stress that it is essentially fictional and that the roles are not modelled on any real-life people – which is why we have set it in the future rather than the past. The intentions of the game are:

- that participants should experience something of the costs and benefits – the negative and positive effects – of conflict, in this case community conflict;
- that they should develop skills in negotiating conflict, and in problem-solving; and
- that they should be able to analyse feedback and use the results to develop techniques for negotiating crisis.

Scenario:
Summary of Events Sheet
This is a summary of the crisis as reported in the *Bathurst Chronicle*, May 12 2009.

Tuesday May 6: gangs of motorbike riders began to arrive in Bathurst (normal population, 25,000) in their hundreds. They camped out on Mount Panorama, drinking heavily.

107

There has always been some trouble with drunken spectators during the motorbike races in past years; but their behaviour this time was the worst yet. There are hundreds of acres of bushland on the mountain – police cannot patrol it all.

Wednesday May 7: there are now several thousand campers on Mount Panorama, mostly members of bike gangs living rough in the bush. A few of them beat up some students from the nearby university as they were walking home across a field at the foot of Mount Panorama. One student was kicked in the head and may suffer permanent brain damage.

Thursday May 8: the police paid several visits to the makeshift campsite of the bikers but made no arrests. A representative from the student union accused police of neglect of duty. This representative claimed that the local chamber of commerce supported the presence of the bikers because they spent money in the town at a time of general economic downturn. The student representative further accused the chamber of commerce of putting pressure on the police to 'go easy' with the troublemakers.

Friday May 9: twelve students were attacked in three separate incidents. They described their attackers as bikers who had claimed to be 'kicking the gays off the campus'. However, no arrests were made except for two students who were booked for possession of marijuana.

Saturday May 10: two days before the race. Police raided the biker campsite from the police base on Mount Panorama, an enclosure surrounded by a high steel-mesh fence with locked gates for security. The bikers turned the tables on the police by locking them into this compound, jeering and throwing stones at them for an hour until reinforcements arrived and drove them off. No arrests were made. Police officers argued that in the darkness it was impossible to tell attackers from innocent campers.

Monday May 12: a public holiday and the day of the race. The race took place peacefully; there were no more demonstrations among the 10,000 spectators, and local community fundraisers such as the Lions Club and the football clubs did a roaring trade selling food and drink from booths and stalls on the mountain – as did local retailers who sold T-shirts and other souvenirs. In the evening as hundreds of bikers roared off through the town they shouted threats to bomb the university on their return next year.

Time required to play TOWN AND GOWN: about two hours.
Number of players: at least nine - that is, at least four groups of two people and one reporter.
Materials:

- a summary of events for each group (as above);
- role instructions and additional information for each group (as below);
- signs and name tags in four colours to designate the different groups.

You will need a room large enough for the four groups and the reporter(s) to sit at tables on their own; and a table with four chairs in the middle of the room for the representatives' meetings.
Roles: assemble players into four groups (representing the university academic board; the staff and student associations; townspeople; and police) and one or two reporters. Get everybody seated at their respective tables and give them each a copy of the summary of events and their various roles as representatives of:

- the university academic board (group 1);
- the university academic staff association (group 2);
- the university student union (group 2);
- the local chamber of commerce (group 3);
- the city guild (group 3);
- the police (group 4);
- the local and national press (group 5).

Ask the reporter(s) to make notes during the negotiations and share them during debriefing. If you want to video the game, the camera will represent TV coverage of the event.
Rules: give groups their role information and additional information and let them discuss their strategies for about 20 minutes. Then hold the first meeting in the middle of the room, between a representative from each group (a minimum of four

people: everybody else becomes an observer). Make sure the speakers talk loudly enough to be heard by everybody in the room.

Allow them to negotiate for about 15 to 20 minutes. Then send them back to their respective corners to confer with their colleagues – after which there is a second round of negotiation.

Notes for debriefing

After the game, ask each group to describe its pre-negotiation decisions and how these affected the progress of the meeting. Explore the hidden agendas and identify who had the most power in this situation and why. Did any benefits result from this community conflict? If so, what were they? What strategies, tactics and manoeuvres did the various negotiators employ? What did this game 'teach' participants about conflict resolution?

Role instructions, group 1

Your group consists of members of the academic board. You are here to discuss plans for a meeting this afternoon between your representatives and those of the university academic staff association and the university student union; the local chamber of commerce and the city guild (a group of concerned and conservative townspeople with considerable local influence); and the police. Local and national press journalists will be present (and there may be TV coverage).

The object of the meeting is to try and avoid a mass student protest planned to be held on the steps of the chancellery next week with the full support of the academic staff union who have threatened to go on strike if the motorbike race is not cancelled next year. The students may decide to march on the town, in which case the demo may become violent. There are likely to be ugly clashes between students and townspeople, the latter being generally in favour of keeping the race.

Additional information, group 1

Because of the recent bad publicity over the motorbike races, an increasing number of parents have been pressing for better protection of their young people at this residential university. Most students live on campus. A significant number of students have withdrawn or been withdrawn by their parents. Student attendance at lectures and tutorials has fallen dramatically. Student morale is low and university counsellors have reported an increasing number of student clients. However, most of these students are not fee-paying (they are on government grants) and many of them have caused a great deal of trouble administratively because of their radical behaviour.

This campus has only recently achieved university status – it was formerly a college of advanced education. The new vice-chancellor is very anxious that the university should be market-oriented in order to attract increasing numbers of full-fee-paying (and more conservative) students. Moroever, many long-term academic staff members – though they have a proven track record – are poorly qualified by university standards. Ideally, you would like to replace them as well.

You are indifferent to the issue of the motorbike race per se but you are interested in its implications for university politics. The local police have refused to take responsibility for handling the demo, arguing this is a matter for campus security and university administration. If you do not prevent the demo, a number of your more radical students and staff will probably end up in serious trouble – which will probably give you sufficient grounds for getting rid of them. But at what price?

Role instructions, group 2

You are representatives of the university academic staff association and the student union. You are here to discuss plans for a meeting this afternoon between yourselves and representatives of the university academic board; the local chamber of commerce and the city guild (a group of concerned and conservative townspeople with considerable local influence); and the police. Local and national press journalists will be present (and there may be TV coverage).

The object of the meeting is that the chamber of commerce and the police want to persuade you to call off a mass student and staff protest you plan to hold on the steps of the chancellery next week. The student union has the full support of the academic staff association which has threatened to take its members out on strike if the motorbike race is not cancelled next year. You are all aware that the students feel very strongly on this matter and that the demo could well become violent if they march on the town and clash with the townspeople who are in favour of keeping the race.

Additional information, group 2

Because of the recent bad publicity over the motorbike race and the attacks on students, an increasing number of parents have been pressing for better protection of their young people at this residential university. Most students live on campus. A significant number of students have withdrawn or been withdrawn by their parents. Student attendance at lectures and tutorials has fallen dramatically. Student morale is low and university counsellors have reported an increasing number of student clients. You are aware there will be talk of staff retrenchments if this situation continues.

This campus has only recently achieved university status – it was formerly a college of advanced education – and many long-term academic staff members, though they have a proven track record, are poorly qualified by university standards. This makes them particularly vulnerable if there are to be cutbacks.

To what extent will the demo, if it is allowed to continue, aggravate this situation? On the other hand, will students continue to be at risk if the bike races take place next year?

You are also aware the student protest is being fuelled by anti-bike conservationist agitators and members of militant neo-fascist groups from the city.

Role instructions, group 3

Your group consists of members of the local chamber of commerce and the city guild, which is a group of concerned and active local residents with considerable local influence. You are here to discuss plans for a meeting this afternoon between your representatives and those of the university academic board; the university academic staff association and the students' union; and the local police. Local and national press journalists will be present (and there may be TV coverage).

The object of the meeting is to try and avoid a mass student protest planned to be held on the steps of the chancellery next week with the full support of the academic staff union who have threatened to go on strike if the motorbike race is not cancelled next year. The students may decide to march on the town, in which case the demo may become violent. There are likely to be ugly clashes between students and townspeople, who are generally in favour of keeping the race.

It is very important to you to find a way to keep the university and students happy while retaining the bike race in Bathurst next year. The benefits to the town of the race far outweigh the costs. For nearly a week each year, because of the race, thousands of extraordinarily dressed and flamboyant visitors flood into the town, spending money like water and doing no damage at all to the town itself. Not only are tourists and other visitors attracted to the area to watch the race, but many others come for the colourful spectacle as a whole. Moreover the fact that this international race is held at Mount Panorama puts Bathurst 'on the map' for millions of Australians and overseas visitors who would never otherwise have heard of it – which is good for tourism in general.

Additional information, group 3

You are aware that the police have refused to take responsibility for the demonstration. They argue it is entirely a matter for campus security and university administration. However, the police have informed you that they have good reason to believe student protest is being fuelled by anti-bike agitators and members of militant conservation groups from the city.

Role instructions, group 4

You represent the local police. You are here to discuss plans for a meeting this afternoon between your representatives and those of the university academic board; the university academic staff association and the university students' union; and the chamber of commerce and the city guild (a group of conservative, concerned and influential local citizens). Local and national press journalists will be present (and there will be TV coverage).

The object of the meeting is to try and avoid a mass student protest planned to be held on the steps of the chancellery next week with the full support of the academic staff union who have threatened to go on strike if the motorbike race is not cancelled next year. The students may decide to march on the town, in which case the demo may become violent. There are likely to be ugly clashes between students and townspeople, who are generally in favour of keeping the race.

You have refused to become involved with this demonstration, arguing that it is a purely campus matter and controlling it is up to campus security and university administration. On the whole, you like the students. They give very little trouble, whereas the bike races have been a police nightmare for years.

You are aware that for the bulk of the townspeople, the benefits of the race far outweigh the costs. For nearly a week each year, because of the race, thousands of extraordinarily dressed and flamboyant visitors flood into the town, spending money like water and doing no damage at all to the town itself. Not only are people attracted to the area who want to watch the race, but many others come for the colourful spectacle as a whole. Moreover, the fact that this international race is held at Mount Panorama puts Bathurst 'on the map' for millions of Australians and overseas visitors who would never otherwise have heard of it – which is good for tourism in general.

You have been under considerable local pressure in the past to turn a blind eye to minor misdemeanours by race visitors. You have done your best to resist this pressure but, in consequence, relations have sometimes been rather strained between you and the town. If there really is some kind of violent demonstration between townspeople and students, the results will be very bad for police public relations.

Additional information, group 4

You have passed on information to the university and the chamber of commerce that you have good reason to believe the demo is being fuelled by city-based militants from a conservationist group that has been trying for years to make motorbike racing illegal. Privately, you have tried to make arrangements for out-of-town police reserves to be inconspicuously present in the town in case the students decide to march; but this has proved impossible. There has been a recent breakout of several maximum-security prisoners from the local prison and all available police officers are engaged in the effort to recapture them.

Role instructions, group 5: the press

You represent the local and national press (and possibly TV coverage). You are here to report on a meeting this afternoon between representatives of the university academic board; the university staff association and the university students' union; the chamber of commerce and the city guild (a group of concerned, conservative and influential local citizens); and the police.

The object of the meeting is to try and avoid a mass student protest planned to be held on the steps of the chancellery next week with the full support of the academic staff union who have threatened to go on strike if the motorbike race is not cancelled next year. The students may decide to march on the town, in which case the demo may become violent. There are likely to be ugly clashes between students and townspeople, who are generally in favour of keeping the race.

Additional information, group 5

As far as you are concerned, the newsworthy aspects of this situation are as follows:

- The townspeople want to keep the race. Not only are sporting fans attracted, but many others come for the colourful spectacle as a whole.
- The fact that this international race is held at Mount Panorama puts Bathurst 'on the map' for millions of Australians and overseas visitors who would never otherwise have heard of it – which is good for tourism in general.
- Because of the attacks on students by bikers this year, the university will logically want the race to be banned. The campus has only recently achieved university status – it was formerly a college of advanced education. It is presumably anxious to keep its new image brightly polished; and therefore may have a strong vested interest in controlling its more radical elements, both student and staff.
- There is a rumour that the student protest is being fuelled by anti-bike agitators and members of militant conservation groups from the city.
- The police have refused to take responsibility for the

demonstration. They argue it is entirely a matter for campus security and university administration.

- There has been a recent breakout of several maximum-security prisoners from the local prison and all available police officers are engaged in the effort to recapture them. This means that if there is a violent demonstration in town the police possibly would not be able to control it immediately.

YO SOY BEAN: a simulation about attitudes in negotiation

The extent of someone's control over a situation usually depends to some degree on their attitude towards that situation and its various components. In negotiation, however skilful the participants, they will handicap themselves if they adopt negative attitudes that prevent them from developing a good working relationship with the other party or parties. Likewise, the negotiation will also suffer if there are personality clashes or if any of the disputants has a particular bias against the topic under discussion.

Of course, people will also disadvantage themselves by taking too positive an attitude towards a particular negotiation. If, for instance, you are an Australian executive who has spent a lot of time in Japan, you may find yourself so attracted to the people and the culture that you are prejudiced in their favour. This works against you when bargaining with your Japanese opposite number. On the other hand if you are an Australian business manager who dislikes the Japanese and has little patience with people who don't speak English the same way you do ('bloody foreigners!') – or if you adopt the attitude that you're doing them a favour because you don't really need overseas markets anyway – then these attitudes will probably prevent your agreement to any kind of business deal with a Japanese company, however attractive the offer.

Likewise, as an employer, if you feel resentful towards trade unions in general, if you think all shop stewards are aggressive troublemakers and that you shouldn't have to negotiate at all over working conditions because you're the one who pays the wages, then you're not likely to experience smooth industrial relations. Moreover, a frustrated or hostile attitude might make you want to score points off the opposition at the expense of the negotiation – for example, trying to make people lose face by bargaining over positions when you should be concentrating on the overall interests of both yourself and the other party. Effective negotiators focus on issues, not positions - which is what this next game is designed to illustrate.

Fisher and Ury in *Getting to Yes* (1988) point out that in most negotiations people commonly engage in positional bargaining. Each side adopts an attitude ('I want delivery by the end of the month'), argues for it and makes concessions to reach a compromise. Yet every negotiation should ideally be based on three criteria that have nothing to do with attitudes:

- it should end in an agreement that as far as possible meets the legitimate interests of each side;
- it should resolve conflicting interests fairly and in a durable fashion;
- it should be socially responsible, and should improve or at least not damage the relationship between the parties.

When negotiators strike attitudes over positions, their egos become involved. They risk losing face by changing position and so the negotiation becomes a power struggle with everybody stating what they will or will not do and failing to listen to anybody else. These attitudes are potentially dangerous to the relationship between the parties. But, as suggested above, it is equally dangerous to be so concerned with the relationship that you give up taking a position at all. If you look at negotiation as a series of transactions between people whose egos are constantly moving between adult, parent and child states of mind (Berne 1984), then the secret of effective negotiation is for the parties to stop behaving as 'parents' and 'children' and start behaving like adults by:

- separating the people from the problem;
- focusing on interests, not positions;
- considering as many options as possible, before focusing on one;
- using objective standards to judge the results.

There is one more point about attitudes to bear in mind when you debrief YO SOY BEAN below: an attitude of belief in one's case is also important (Fowler 1986:92). For example if one or more players found it difficult to hold convincingly to a position or argument adopted by their team because they felt it to be illogical or unfair, you can remind them that in real life these ethical questions need to be considered in the pre-negotiation, planning phase. That is the time to investigate team members' attitudes and perceptions, rather than discovering in the middle of the negotiation that they were overly negative or positive towards the opposition.

YO SOY BEAN was originally designed for a group of American sales managers from Iowa, to practise bargaining with Japanese buyers to sell large quantities of soybean (hence the name of the game). It has proved equally effective as a monocultural negotiation exercise for private and public sector American, Australian and British players. It appears to be generally effective for conveying basic information about the ways in which participants' attitudes towards each other, the other parties to the negotiation and the task itself will materially affect negotiation outcomes. It is also a good game for videotaping.

Time required: at least one hour to play and about the same time to debrief.
Number of players: any number from two upwards, but the game seems to work most effectively with six to ten players. If numbers are larger, people can be put into several negotiating teams and you can hold a session afterwards for them to compare notes.
Materials:

- ordinary classroom materials including a whiteboard, blackboard or flipboard to record your comments and those of the observers (if observers are present);
- a personal computer (PC) with keyboard, monitor and any word-processing software with which you are familiar. You will find a printer useful too, not because you need it for the game, but because players often ask for a hard copy of the computer entries. If you have no computer or keyboard skills you will have to include somebody who has.

Scenario and roles: you will play the role of interpreter. The rest of the players represent members of two negotiation teams, each with a team leader (except for two or three observers, if the group is large enough to allow for them; observers should take written notes on the progress of the game).

Seat the teams as far apart as possible and give each one an imaginary nationality – one can be from Mars and the other from Terra, or wherever. Give the information below to everybody.

The team from Terra represents a company that wants to sell a large consignment of soybean which the team from Mars wants to buy. The following now needs to be negotiated:

- the quantity of soybean to be bought;
- delivery (date, place, method);
- price and method of payment.

Though the Martians are all bilingual (that is, they speak and understand English in addition to their own language), they have requested that Martian shall be the language of the conference table on alternate days with English, which is the Terrestrials' national language (days will be represented by 15-minute periods).

The Terrestrials are monolingual, therefore it will be necessary to call in an interpreter on the days when the Martians will be speaking nothing but Martian. On these days the Martian team will communicate with the Terrestrials by having the team leader key messages into the computer. The Martians and the interpreter are the only people who can see the monitor screen. When the team leader has finished typing, the interpreter (you) will sit at the computer and read aloud what is on the screen. The Terrestrials will reply verbally but the Martians will not respond until the interpreter has typed the message on to the screen. They then discuss its contents among themselves by scribbling notes to each other. The leader sits at the computer and types the answer. The interpreter then takes the leader's place and reads out the reply ... and so on until the Martian-speaking time period is up. Everybody reverts to English for the next period and neither computer nor interpreter are needed.

You may or may not want to stipulate that the negotiators have previously agreed the negotiation may include other products. In any case, the above sequence continues until everybody has had enough or you run out of time.

It becomes apparent immediately that the Martians are being deliberately obstructive because though they can speak and understand English, at times they pretend not to be able to; presumably the reason is that they want to gain an unfair edge over the Terrestrials. Just how they and the Terrestrials handle this situation is up to the players. The game is also frustrating, particularly for the Terrestrials, because they have to wait for the interpretation process each time there is an interchange with the Martians. Since the game is designed to explore the effects of negative attitudes on negotiation, this frustration is something that players should be encouraged to talk about afterwards.

Rules: seat the two negotiating teams opposite each other, at separate tables as far apart as possible. There should be at least one observer for each group if there is more than one pair of negotiating teams. Remember, you need a computer and somebody who knows how to use the word-processor software for each negotiation.

When you've issued everybody with the scenario and apportioned the general information and the respective team role cards, give players at least five minutes to read and absorb everything, and to ask any procedural questions. Then give both teams about ten minutes (or longer if you think they need more time) for pre-negotiation, to discuss their strategy in private. Send them away somewhere to do this while you set up the computer(s) and have a quiet chat with the other interpreters if there are any.

Call everybody back. When they are all settled and any last-minute procedural questions have been asked and answered briefly, negotiation can begin. The two delegation leaders toss a coin to determine whether English or Martian shall begin the negotiation for the first 15 minutes. Tell everybody you will indicate when it is time to switch. Add that any behaviour is permissible so long as it is legitimate in the context of the game's scenario. From then on, don't interfere at all. If Martians or Terrestrials ask to leave the room to 'consult with head office', permit this. When time is up, call a halt and take stock of the situation. Post a summary statement of the stage the negotiation has reached.

Monitoring the game: if you don't want to video YO SOY BEAN or don't have the facilities, you really need neutral observers to take notes so they can contribute something concrete to the debrief.

You can provide them with a checklist of attitudes if you like. The players will realize quite quickly that of course the negotiation would be much easier if everybody spoke English all the time; so why isn't this happening? The most obvious reason appears to be that the Martians have adopted an attitude of suspicion regarding the Terrestrials' good faith, therefore they want at least some periods of time during which they can confer with each other before writing their reply.

If the Terrestrials come to this conclusion (and they usually do), this will affect their own attitude towards the Martians and the kind of positions they take up. For example, they may demand the removal of the computer and independent interpreter and assert that in fact one of their own team members is bilingual and will act as interpreter. Whatever objections they make the negotiation will be in danger of becoming blocked while the two teams argue about the way it is set up.

Because the negotiation environment of YO SOY BEAN is designed to evoke conflict – or at least misunderstanding – the attitude of the negotiators is likely to be one of attack rather than a desire to build a relationship that will let them get on with the job. Interestingly, players' attitudes sometimes become more coopera- tive through the original cause of dispute: the computer. Both teams become engrossed in talking to each other via the computer and virtually lose sight of their respective goals – recollecting them only on your warning that the game is nearly over. Then these players frequently sink their differences and negotiate to high mutual benefit in the last five minutes. If this happens you can make the point afterwards that if bargainers will agree to focus on mutual interests rather than power positions or other subjective criteria, a great deal can be accomplished satisfactorily in a very short time.

Information for Terrestrials only

You represent a state-funded agency which is attempting to coordinate the efforts of soybean farmers all over the planet. You want urgently to sell 1000 tons of soybean at ten yin per ton before the crop goes rotten and hundreds of farmers go broke. For the sake of the farmers' livelihood you want immediate payment in full from the Martians on their receipt of the consignment. You are not fussy about the exact date you are required to deliver the goods, provided it is within the next two or three months, but you want the Martians to accept delivery in a single consignment. Freight will have to be by spaceship, but you want the Martians to take delivery from the dock and make their own arrangement for the subsequent transport within their own planet. You have secret information that the Martians' potato crop failed disastrously this year and they are likely to be desperate to buy your soybean to feed their people.

Information for Martians only

The staple food of your planet is potatoes but a blight seriously affected the crop this year and your people are facing a serious food shortage which could become a country-wide famine. You desperately need to buy soybean from the Terrestrials as a substitute for potato but can only afford 500 tons of soybean at eight yin per ton. You want a staggered delivery of 100 tons per month over the next three months, paying for each delivery as it arrives. Freight will be by spaceship and you want the Terrestrials to be responsible for this. You are very suspicious of the Terrestrials. You have demanded that your language be used half of the time even though you speak and understand English quite well. You have done this in order to have more time to consult with one another before making any replies to the Terrestrials' proposals.

MONUMENTAL

MONUMENTAL is designed to illustrate how the personalities of the negotiators will affect the demands that are made, the claims staked and the concessions offered in negotiation. It is derivative of many similar exercises. Its only special claims are that the theatricality of the role names often seems to encourage players to behave more extrovertly than they might otherwise do – which is good for the dynamics of the game. The players are constrained to behave as real-life managers in that they have to handle a variety of tasks simultaneously.

Time required: at least two hours, but the game can run for longer if this suits your purposes.

Number of players: MONUMENTAL can be played with as few as five people. If there are more than five, you can organize more than one conference. Each group confers separately and everybody can compare notes later. If there are fewer than five people per conference you can try omitting one or more roles but the results may not be as effective as with larger numbers. Our advice is to stick to five players or multiples of five and ask any extras to be observers.

Materials:

- One rolecard for each player and a name tag to go with it.
- Several hundred plastic drinking straws in green, red and yellow. If you can't get these colours, you will have to alter the relevant role instructions. You can also use interlocking building bricks of coloured plastic, or any other model-building materials that you commonly use in games of this sort. There is an astonishing variety of building kits available nowadays in toy shops, their only disadvantage being that they are expensive. If you are charging a large fee as a consultant to run negotiation workshops this may not be a relevant factor.
- Three boxes of long pins (not tiny dressmaker pins) if you use straws as building material.
- A set of interruption cards, which you will hand one at a time to individual players at intervals during the game. Distribute them frequently and choose moments when your victims are fully occupied with the game.
- A telephone instrument (real or toy) to go with one of the interruption cards.
- Tables and chairs for the teams.
- Writing materials for all players.

Scenario: a conference room in which several people have met to decide the design of a sculpture for the new and prestigious premises of a large government department. The materials for the sculpture are represented by coloured drinking straws and pins (or whatever). Conference members discuss the details of a miniature prototype to determine the shape, colour and cost of the finished work. The conflicting interests of the various negotiators make agreement difficult. Demands have to give way to concessions if the whole project is not to collapse. An immediate decision is essential if the sculpture is to be finished before the visit of the prime minister who will give final agreement to the sculpture (or withold it).

Roles: the players represent the following characters:

- Pat Artcraft, CEO of a design company, Designs for Open Spaces. This company has the contract to build the sculpture.
- Mat (Matthew or Matilda) McMean, a representative from the government's finance department, who will decide the cost of the sculpture.
- Sam (or Samantha) Scratch, the sales manager of Pins Unlimited, the company that will provide the construction pins for the sculpture.
- Jill (or Jack) Straw, the owner of a company called Straw's Castle, that manufactures and sells the building straws that will be used for the sculpture.
- Sir (or Lady) Hilary Vainglory, the permanent head of the government department.

Rules:

- Organize the players into groups of five people, each group seated at a separate table.
- Explain the setting (as described above) or give them each a written copy.
- Allocate the roles. Don't duplicate – for example by giving Pat Artcraft an assistant – until all five have been taken. Introduce the characters to each other and explain the reason for each one's presence at the conference. Give each a large name-tag to wear.
- Issue samples of building materials (at least 50 straws in the three colours and one packet of pins per table).
- Give players about five minutes to absorb their role instructions. Answer any procedural questions, then set the timer for half an hour and let the players get on with building the prototype and negotiating its colours and cost.
- At frequent intervals, hand an interruption card to a player and make sure they follow the instructions on the card.
- Together with any other observers, make written notes of any

behaviour you would like to discuss afterwards with the players, particularly relating to concessions and demands.

● Stop the game after about 20 minutes and initiate a discussion, based on your notes. Then ask the players to continue in role and take the negotiation further. Keep stopping them and debriefing the action every 20 minutes or so.

Rolecards

Jack (or Jill) Straw, owner of Straw's Castle. Your company manufactures and sells building straws. You are at a conference to decide the details of a sculpture for the forecourt of a new government building. It has been agreed that the sculpture will be made from your straws, but conference members still have to agree on colours and costs. You are with: Pat Artcraft, CEO of a design company, Designs for Open Spaces, the company which has the contract to build the sculpture; Mat (Matthew or Matilda) McMean, a representative from the government's finance department, who will decide the cost of the sculpture; Sam (or Samantha) Scratch, the sales manager of Pins Unlimited, the company that will provide the construction pins for the sculpture; and Sir (or Lady) Hilary Vainglory, the permanent head of the government department.

You do a lot of business with all these people, and don't want to alienate any of them. The task of the conference is to agree on the design of a miniature prototype of the sculpture, with straws you have provided, of one-tenth the size of the real thing. In other words, if the model contains 50 straws on completion, the sculpture will require 500. Your final price will depend on the selected colours as well as their numbers.

You would like the sculpture to contain as many green straws as possible. Apart from their being the most profitable, you have them in large quantities. You definitely do not want yellow used in any quantity, since these straws would be very difficult, if not impossible, to provide. At present, your supply of yellow straws has run rather low because the dye makers have had difficulty providing you with this colour, owing to its popularity with their other customers. You have plenty of green straws and adequate supplies of the red.

Your prices are as follows: green straws: $100 each, with a 10 per cent discount for orders over 100; red straws: $75 each, with a discount as above; and yellow straws: $60 each, with a discount as above.

Pins Unlimited's prices are as follows: 10 pins: $100; 20 pins: $150; 30 pins: $200; 40 pins: $250; 50 pins: $300.

Pat Artcraft, Head of Designs for Open Spaces. Your company, Designs for Open Spaces, has obtained a contract to design a sculpture for the forecourt of a new government building. The ministry has awarded contracts for provision of building materials to two companies: Straw's Castle and Pins Unlimited. Jack Straw's prices are as follows: green straws: $100 each, with a 10 per cent discount for orders over 100; red straws: $75 each, with a discount as above; and yellow straws: $60 each, with a discount as above.

Pins Unlimited's prices are as follows: 10 pins: $100; 20 pins: $150; 30 pins: $200; 40 pins: $250; 50 pins: $300.

You are now in conference with: Jack (or Jill) Straw and Sam (Samuel or Samantha) Scratch, the respective sales directors of the above two companies; a government representative, Mat (Matthew or Matilda) McMean, to advise on costing and other guidelines; and Sir (or Lady) Hilary Vainglory, the head of the department whose building will be the site of the sculpture.

The task of the conference is to agree on the design of a miniature prototype of the sculpture, with pins and straws provided by the respective suppliers, of one-tenth the size of the real thing. In other words, if the model contains 50 straws and 50 pins on completion, the sculpture will require 500 of each. You are aware of the need to strike a balance between art and expense. McMean is known to you as a skinflint who will cut costs to the bone on the slightest excuse; on the other hand Vainglory will want something impressive; and you do a lot of business with Straw and Scratch – you value their good relations.

Sam (Samuel or Samantha) Scratch, sales director of Pins Unlimited. Your company manufactures construction pins, and your prices are as follows; 10 pins: $100; 20 pins: $150; 30 pins: $200; 40 pins: $250; 50 pins: $300; over 50: subject to negotiation.

You have been awarded a contract to supply pins for the construction of a sculpture for the foyer of a new government building. You are now in conference with Pat Artcraft, the head of the design company, Designs for Open Spaces, which is to build it. The other people present at the conference are: Jack or Jill Straw, the owner of Straw's Castle, the company that will provide the construction straws; Mat (or Matilda) McMean, a government representative to advise on costing; and Sir (or Lady) Hilary Vainglory, the permanent head of the government department whose foyer will hold the finished sculpture.

The task of the conference is to agree on the design of a miniature prototype of the sculpture, with pins you have provided, of one-tenth the size of the real thing. In other words, if the model contains 50 pins on completion, the sculpture will require 500.

As well as protecting your own interests at this conference, you have a hidden agenda. You have taken a commission from Never Say Never Say Dye (NSNSD) to push for as many yellow and red straws as possible in the design of the sculpture.

Mat (or Matilda) McMean, government representative. The government has awarded the following contracts: to Designs for Open Spaces, to design a sculpture for the forecourt of a new government department building; to Straw's Castle and Pins Unlimited, respectively, for provision of construction straws and pins.

Jack Straw's prices are as follows: red straws: $100 each, with a 10 per cent discount for orders over 100; green straws: $75 each, with a discount as above; and yellow straws: $60 each, with a discount as above.

Pins Unlimited's prices are as follows: 10 pins: $100; 20 pins: $150; 30 pins: $200; 40 pins: $250; 50 pins: $300.

You are now in conference with Pat Artcraft of Designs for Open Spaces, Jack (or Jill) Straw of Straw's Castle, Sam (or Samantha) Scratch of Pins Unlimited, and Sir (or Lady) Hilary Vainglory, the permanent head of the department whose building will be the site of the sculpture.

The task of the conference is to agree on the design of a miniature prototype of the sculpture, with pins and straws provided by the respective suppliers, of one-tenth the size of the real thing. In other words, if the model contains 50 straws and 50 pins on completion, the sculpture will require 500 of each.

Your brief is to keep costs as low as possible. You are proud of your reputation of being a skinflint and as far as you are concerned the sculpture should be made entirely of yellow straws and as small as is reasonably acceptable.

Sir (or Lady) Hilary Vainglory. The government has awarded the following contracts: to Designs for Open Spaces, to design a sculpture for the forecourt of a new building which will house the government department of which you are the permanent secretary; to Straw's Castle and Pins Unlimited, respectively, for provision of construction straws and pins.

Straw's prices are as follows: red straws: $100 each, with a 10 per cent discount for orders over 100; green straws: $75 each, with a discount as above; and yellow straws: $60 each, with a discount as above.

Pins Unlimited's prices are as follows: 10 pins: $100; 20 pins: $150; 30 pins: $200; 40 pins: $250; 50 pins: $300.

You are now in conference with the managing director of Designs for Open Spaces, and the sales directors of the two suppliers. Also present is a government representative to advise on costing and other guidelines.

The task of the conference is to agree on the design of a miniature prototype of the sculpture, with pins and straws provided by the respective suppliers, of one-tenth the size of the real thing. In other words, if the model contains 50 straws and 50 pins on completion, the sculpture will require 500 of each.

You will retire soon, and as far as you are concerned, the sculpture will be a personal monument to your lifetime of government service. You want it to be as large, substantial and handsome as possible. You don't like the colour green.

Interruption card

You are called away on urgent business. Drop out of the conference and become an observer for five minutes.

Interruption card

The Prime Minister is on the telephone. Improvise an imaginary telephone conversation with the PM for five minutes (the messenger will time you).

Interruption card

A parcel arrives for you COD. You need its contents urgently but have to find five pounds to pay for it. The messenger will not leave without the money and you cannot rejoin the conference until you have paid the money.

Interruption card

The shop that does all your printing is threatening to refuse you further service unless you pay their outstanding account which seems to have been overlooked by your department. Find five pounds and give it to the game director, who represents the printing firm and who won't leave you in peace until you find the money.

Interruption card

A sample is required urgently for a client for whom you design clothing items. Find a piece of red material from somewhere and give it to the game director.

Interruption card

An advertisement for your company has given offence to some newspaper readers. Find a copy of today's newspaper and give it to the game director to be checked.

Interruption card

The photocopy machine has broken down in your office. Give the game director instructions about the bulk copying that has to be done before 5pm today.

Interruption card

One of your support staff has just fainted in your office. The game leader wants to know what to do.

No doubt you can think of other interruptions for the players. The object of each is to distract recipients and force them to deal with irrelevant but time-consuming matters that require concentration and distract them from the 'real' negotiation. Ask them afterwards how they felt about these interruptions and help them to relate this experience to a typical day in the life of a manager. Managers are said to be people who are never able to concentrate on anything for more than about 20 minutes before being interrupted to deal with something else.

BUSINESS SCHOOL: A simulation about negotiation of conflict
The topic could also be called 'constructive compromise' because this game deals with the handling of conflict within a management team – always a matter of delicate compromise. Moreover, the participants handle it themselves without any help from you, until your discussion with them after the game. BUSINESS SCHOOL is an effective exercise for syndicates to work through in their own time during a conference, workshop, residential seminar etc.

(*Note:* When you prepare handouts to go with this game, each section must be on a separate sheet.)

The original concept is not our own. We wish we could remember where we got it from because then we could acknowledge its creator. All game leaders accumulate an enormous amount of material from a very wide range of sources: they play around with it, reshape and rewrite it, until its origins become obscured by the mists of time. The debt that simulation gamers owe each other is incalculable.

Time: at least two hours.
Participants: any number, divided into groups of three to seven people.
Materials: none, except the following 22 sections beginning below, under 'Handout'. Give a copy of these instructions to each participant when you introduce the exercise and form the groups. After that, they're on their own.

Handout

Section 1: Scenario
This simulation asks you to imagine you are a lecturer in the School of Business at Anon University, teaching management studies as part of a bachelor of business degree. Students' assignments are marked not only by you but also by a team of casual, part-time tutors from elsewhere. Therefore, careful quality control of marking standards is essential. Before all the marks for each assignment can be confirmed by the professor and turned over to the student centre for formal recording, they must pass through your quality control check. Each tutor must submit for your inspection an example of a student's assignment to which they have awarded an A, a B and a C respectively; it is your job to make sure they are all marking consistently. If not, you have to scale their marks up or down as the case may be, in order to be fair to all students.

From time to time you meet with problems, and when this happens you usually discuss them first with your peer-level lecturers in the school whose work is linked to yours. In the past this strategy has worked well and benefited everybody.

Section 2: Roles
In this game you will compete with other teams and even colleagues within your own team to achieve the best performance: that is, a climate in which disagreement can be handled most effectively. Personal as well as group decisions will be called for. Usually you will be asked to decide a problem for yourself first, and then to discuss your ideas with your teammates to achieve a group consensus.

Group decisions can be made by majority vote, but consensus is desirable if possible – though your two-hour time limit may constrain you to accept a majority decision. A major purpose of the game is to stimulate discussion of the various approaches to conflict resolution that team members find successful. For scoring purposes, some answers will be more 'right' than others, but this does not mean they are always the best solutions in every case in real life. In the final analysis you do not win this game on the basis of your game score, but on the number of useful ideas you take away from it.

Section 3: Worksheet

This worksheet is to record your decisions and scores. *Do not write on it until you are asked to do so.*

Keep the worksheet separate – its contents, when you fill it, are personal and for your eyes only.

Line	Phase	Personal		Group		Votes
		choice	score	choice	score	
1	I: Facing the conflict					
2	II: Approaching the prof	a)				
		b)				
3	III: Recognizing emotional reactions					
4	IV: Anticipating emotional reactions					
5	V: Opening communication					
6	VI. Defusing conflict					
7	VII: Creating an open communication climate	a)				
		b)				
Total						

Section 4: Instructions

- At each stage of the negotiation, do not read the next section until instructed to do so.
- Once you and your team members have begun a new section, do not go back and change decisions made in a previous section. (However, you may turn back at any time to refresh your memory.)
- When you have finished reading this section (s 4), and taken out the worksheet, turn to the next section.

Game phase I: Facing the conflict

Section 5

This morning you handed a batch of marks to your professor for final checking before sending it down to the student centre. The professor has just come to tell you she has tightened procedures because there have been complaints by some students. She says she has already discussed the matter with the dean of the school (to whom you both report) who agrees with her decision. The batch of marks you sent her will have to be rechecked because the tutors will each have to submit not three sample assignments but six: that is, two A-quality assignments, two Bs and two Cs. You know this will involve you and them in a massive amount of extra work because you will have to go back again through all the marked assignments, sort them out according to tutor and send them back to the appropriate tutor, who will then have to select three more assignments for submission. These are all external tutors and this re-checking will have to be sent by post. You try to persuade the professor to apply the new rule only to future assignments but she refuses and leaves.

Rechecking the marks for this last assignment will set you and your tutors back at least a week – which will mean that the students' next assignment will not be marked and returned on time. This will cause a great deal of resentment since examinations are just around the corner and students' nerves are becoming frayed. Moreover, you will be involved in extra costs because the tutors will have to be paid for the extra work and this will have to come out of your already meagre budget.

As you reflect on what has happened, you feel very annoyed. Something must be done!

A: You can calm down, return all assignments to the tutors and instruct them to do the extra work; then prepare to deal with angry students when their next assignment is not returned on time.

B: You can write a formal memo to the professor, insisting it is only fair that the new, stricter standards be applied to future assignments.

C: You can go over her head to the dean and try to persuade him with the same argument.

D: You can send the professor a memo, describing in writing what your problems will be if she insists on imposing the new standards on the marked assignments, and ask her to come up with a solution.

E: You can ask her to find a time suitable for you both to sit down together and talk the whole problem through.

F: You can tell her that if she's not prepared to be flexible you will no longer be able to spare one of your tutors, as you have done in the past, to help her with extra marking for other lecturers. This would be a real threat because the school is so short-staffed.

G: You can go to her office right now and insist on having the whole thing out with her.

These are the only possibilities you can think of at present. Contemplate them for a few moments, then turn to section 6.

Section 6

Without discussion with your team members, choose one of the possibilities in section 7 and enter the relevant letter in the appropriate space on line 1 of the worksheet, 'facing the conflict' under the heading 'personal choice'. Try to finish in five minutes.

As soon as all the members of your team have finished, you will all discuss the various possibilities for about five minutes and decide which choice the group as a whole considers the best.

Now enter this group choice on the same line under the heading 'group choice' in the worksheet. Do not make any entries in the score columns until the game calls for you to do so.

When you have entered the letter representing the group decision - but not before - turn to section 8.

Section 7
After reading the following, enter your personal score and the group score respectively in the appropriate boxes for line 1 on the worksheet.

A: If you say nothing and accept full responsibility for overworked tutors and neglected students, delayed assignments and increased costs, you have done nothing to open negotiation with the professor. Similar conflicts may arise in the future if you do not communicate your problems to her.

Enter scores of two points on line 1 for 'personal score' and/or 'group score' if you and/or the group made this choice.

B: A memo to the professor instructing her to apply her standards only to future assignments is likely to offend her. Any step that does not carefully weigh the reactions of the other party to your behaviour contains potential for unnecessary conflict.

Enter scores of two points on line 1 if you and/or the group made this choice.

C: An appeal to the dean can only complicate the situation. It is unlikely he will countermand the professor's instructions and your interference will only cause resentment.

Enter scores of two points on line 1 if you and/or the group made this choice.

D: Requesting a review of the new ruling via a memo to the professor is a good idea in some ways. It is more difficult for her to ignore your problems if you state them in writing; on the other hand a written memo may put her on the defensive more than a verbal discussion.

Enter scores of eight points on line 1 if you and/or the group made this choice.

E: Making an appointment to speak to the professor is probably the best choice. It will give you time to cool down, prepare your arguments and hope to gain her cooperation by explaining in detail the disturbance it will cause to many people if the new rule is applied to assignments already marked.

Enter scores of ten points on line 1 if you and/or the group made this choice.

F: Threatening the professor is not likely to force her to rescind her ruling, and is a dangerous step that will lead to bad relations in the future. Therefore, this solution will not solve your immediate problem.

Enter scores of no points on line 1 if you and/or the group made this choice.

G: An immediate discussion has advantages and disadvantages. While it might open up communication you may be in too emotional a state to negotiate the discussion effectively. Enter scores of three points on line 1 if you and/or the group made this choice. As soon as you have entered your personal and group scores, turn to section 8.

Game phase II: Approaching the professor

Section 8

Assume you have decided on an immediate discussion (confrontation) with the professor. You enter her office and after an exchange of civilities you introduce your problem.

Without consultation with your team members, write out in the space below the first two or three sentences you would use to state the situation. This should take you about five minutes. When all the members of your team have finished, turn to section 9, but not before.

Section 9

Each of you now reads your statement to the group. After everybody has had their turn, the group discusses the problem.

In this exercise you are competing for the votes of your team members. Therefore, present your viewpoint clearly and concisely. At the same time do not forget this is an exercise in the handling of conflict. Express your opinion and choose your words carefully, so they will have maximum impact. Be impersonal and objective but try at the same time to communicate enthusiasm for your ideas. Don't talk too loudly or overdo eye contact. Try to relax so your body language does not communicate tension. Be as persuasive as you can – remember that at least several other members of the team are probably strongly committed to their respective positions and may need considerable persuasion to make them change their minds.

After about 15 minutes, you all vote by secret ballot on a blank sheet of paper for the two statements you liked best of all the arguments (you can vote for your own if you like). For example, your ballot paper may contain the names 'Jane and John' or 'Mary and Peter' or whoever. One member of the team collects the ballots and announces the number of votes for each participant. You should then enter the number of votes *your* statement receives in the appropriate space in line 2a of the worksheet under 'votes'.

Whether your statement received any votes or not, allow yourself *one additional vote* for any of the ideas listed below that were clearly expressed in your statement, even if not in the same words. Enter these additional votes in the 'votes' box on line 2b:

- I'd like to clarify some points about the new ruling and explore with you the problems they have created for me and my tutors. (One vote.)
- I understand the need for more quality control of marking, but I feel that in this first application of the new ruling you could be flexible in considering the problems it has created for my team. (One vote.)
- I am willing to ask my tutors to submit more examples of work already marked, but since I have a tight schedule, a restricted budget and impatient students, I shall need an extra tutor – without charge to my budget – to mark the next assignment. (One vote.)

- I think the new standards will cause problems for both of us. How about us seeing the dean together to find out if we can relax them a little? (One vote.)

When you have entered your additional votes, if any, proceed to section 10.

Game phase III: Recognizing emotional reactions

Section 10

When you start on this phase of the game, keep in mind that the purpose is to help you review the great complexity of human emotions. An exchange of opinions with the other members of your team should help improve the accuracy and speed with which you can diagnose most potential conflicts – in order either to avoid them or deal with them more effectively.

Imagine how the professor might react to your statement of your problem. For example she might be:

- defensive (justifying her behaviour);
- hostile (accusing or angry, resentful, sullen or withdrawn);
- accepting (non-judgmental, assessing your problem on its merits);
- withdrawing (inclined to avoid your problem, pretending it doesn't exist);
- ready to cooperate in solving the problem by actively participating in the search for a solution.

In section 11 are some typical statements that may reveal her reactions. In the 'personal choice' columns, without discussion with your team members, put a tick in the column opposite each statement that indicates which of the five reactions you think is dominant in it. In fact, the professor's words will probably indicate a mixture of several emotions; try to identify the one you think is the strongest.

Try to finish in five or six minutes. When everybody has ticked their personal choices, you should all discuss the statements and develop group choices. Once these have been made, you can tick them off in the 'group choice' columns. This should take about ten minutes.

Now turn to section 11 and complete the exercise.

Section 11

Note: Def = defensive, hos = hostile, acc = accepting, with = inclined to withdraw, coop = cooperative

	Personal choice					Group choice				
	def	hos	acc	with	coop	def	hos	acc	with	coop
1. I wish you wouldn't involve me. It's your responsibility.										
2. Let's take a closer look at the problem.										
3. I can't help you. The new ruling is necessary, it isn't my fault.										
4. I understand your problem, I'll do what you ask.										
5. I don't mean to upset you, but I have to raise the standard of quality control of marking.										

When everybody has entered the group choices, turn to section 12, but not before.

Section 12: Results

The columns below indicate the most probable interpretations of the statements on the previous page. You will see there is a score of five against each statement both in the 'personal choice' and the 'group choice' columns.

Score your decisions from the previous page by circling, in the 'personal choice' and 'group choice' columns respectively, each number 5 *where the reaction matches the one you (and your group) selected for that particular statement* – remembering there are no absolute answers, only the most likely ones in the circumstances.

Add the circled numbers in each 'choice' column and enter the personal and group totals on line 3 of the worksheet. For example, if your response was that statement 1 and 3 indicated withdrawal and hostility respectively, but none of your other selections matched those below, your total would be ten and you would enter this under 'personal choice' on line 3 of the worksheet.

Type of reaction	Personal score	Group score	
1. Inclined to withdraw	5	5	I wish you wouldn't involve me ...
2. Cooperative	5	5	Let's take a look ...
3. Hostile	5	5	I can't help you ...
4. Accepting	5	5	I understand ...
5. Defensive	5	5	It's no good blaming me ...
Totals			

Game phase IV: Anticipating emotional reactions

Section 13

If the professor reacted to your approach with defensiveness, hostility, acceptance, withdrawal or cooperation, perhaps that is no more than you ought to have expected. What kinds of responses might you expect from her if you opened your discussion with one of the following statements in section 14?

Read them all before making any decisions.

Because people differ, the professor may respond to each statement with any or several of the five reactions suggested in section 14, depending on the type of person she is and the way she sees the situation. Assume, therefore, that some degree of each reaction is possible.

Discuss each of the statements in section 14 with your group and indicate by circling H (high), N (neutral) or L (low) the degree of defensiveness, hostility, acceptance, withdrawal and cooperation with which each statement might be received by the professor. No personal decisions are required here. Try to finish in about ten minutes. When the time is up, or when the group decisions have been recorded in section 14, go on to section 15 – but not before.

Section 14

Note: D = defensive, H = hostile, A = accepting, W = withdrawal, and C = cooperation. H = high reaction, N = neutral reaction, L = low reaction.

D	H	A	W	C	
H	H	H	H	H	**1.** I don't think I can ask my tutors to go through the batch of assignments they've already marked again, though I will tell them about the new rules for quality control from now on. Please ask the dean to make this exception.
N	N	N	N	N	
L	L	L	L	L	
H	H	H	H	H	**2.** I'm always willing to cooperate with you and I always try to do a good job, but I can't cope with recalling all the last batch of marked assignments.
N	N	N	N	N	
L	L	L	L	L	
H	H	H	H	H	**3.** Please let's discuss why we really need these new standards.
N	N	N	N	N	
L	L	L	L	L	
H	H	H	H	H	**4.** I don't think you should have decided to change the quality-control measures for students' assignments without consulting me. I'm in charge of a team of four tutors, with responsibility for the work of nearly 400 students.
N	N	N	N	N	
L	L	L	L	L	
H	H	H	H	H	**5.** These new standards have created a problem for me. I need your help to solve it.
N	N	N	N	N	
L	L	L	L	L	
H	H	H	H	H	**6.** It's not fair to spring new standards on me without letting me know in advance so I can inform my tutors of the new rules.
N	N	N	N	N	
L	L	L	L	L	
H	H	H	H	H	**7.** I'm going to have to ask you to accept this batch of assignments marked to the old quality-control rules. I just don't have the time, and neither do my tutors, to rework the whole batch.
N	N	N	N	N	
L	L	L	L	L	

Section 15

Compare your group's list with the list below. For each answer that matches, allow three points. The scores here, as on other items, are based on the most probable responses and should be accepted in that light. In situations such as the one described, there are obviously no absolutely right or wrong answers, merely more or less correct evaluations. Total the score (maximum 105 points). Enter it on line 4 of the worksheet under 'group score' and go on to section 16.

Note: D = defensive, H = hostile, A = accepting, W = withdrawal, and C = cooperation.

D	H	A	W	C	
H	H	L	H	L	**1.** I don't think I can ask my tutors to go through the batch of assignments they've already marked again, though I will tell them about the new rules for quality control from now on. Please ask the dean to make this exception.
H	H	L	H	L	**2.** I'm always willing to cooperate with you and I always try to do a good job, but I can't cope with recalling all the last batch of marked assignments.
H	L	H	L	N	**3.** Please let's discuss why we really need these new standards.
H	H	L	N	L	**4.** I don't think you should have decided to change the quality-control measures for students' assignments without consulting me.
L	L	N	L	H	**5.** These new standards have created a problem for me. I need your help to solve it.
H	L	H	L	N	**6.** It's not fair to spring new standards on me without letting me know in advance so I can inform my tutors of the new rules.
N	L	L	H	N	**7.** I must ask you to accept this batch of assignments marked to the old rules. I just don't have the time, and neither do my tutors, to rework the whole batch.

For example, if your group's score was:

1: H L H H L = 9 (three responses that match the above)
2: H H L L H = 9 (three matching responses)
3: H L H L N = 15 (all responses match those above)
4: N L H H N = 0 (no matches)
5: L L N L N = 12 (four matches)
6: H H N H H = 3 (one match)
7: H N H N H = 0 (no matches)
Total = 48

Game phase V: Opening communication

Section 16

Now assume you were so annoyed at being asked to rework the marked assignments you could not restrain yourself. You walked in on the professor immediately and told her you needed more consideration. When she said she was just dashing off to a lecture and could not discuss the matter with you now, you reacted angrily. Although you were not openly insulting, you left the clear impression you thought she was doing less than you – and the school – had a right to expect.

In a way, of course, you were right. As team leader, the professor should have been concerned about costs and timetables in the school. You know her to be a proud woman, even arrogant, and it is true she was on her way to give a lecture when you interrupted her. Perhaps if you had approached her differently you might have received a more positive response.

However, what's done is done. Now, what is your best course of action? Again, select from the possibilities below the one that most closely matches what you think you would do in real life. Make your selection without discussing it with your team members.

A: Don't bother about the problem any more – just carry out orders. If she doesn't care about disgruntled and anxious students, why should you? Start thinking instead how you will word a memo to the dean to make sure you are not held accountable for the delays and frustrations you know will result from this new ruling.

B: Write a memo immediately to the professor, restating your original position – that you will comply with the new ruling on quality control of assignment marking, but not for the batch that has just been marked and returned to the students. Ask her again to be flexible about this and describe again the problems it will cause if she persists.

C: Wait until the next day, then see her when she has some free time. Express regret for losing your temper and ask if she can think of a way to solve the problem.

D: Delay talking to her for several days, then call in to her office and reopen the discussion as if nothing had happened.

E: See her as soon as possible and, without apologizing, tell her you have thought the matter over and want to discuss it again with her.

Enter the letter representing your personal choice on line 5 of the worksheet. When all team members have entered their individual choices, you should discuss your selections for five minutes or so and achieve consensus. Each will then enter the group choice on the appropriate line. Then turn to the next section, but not before.

Section 17: Results
Here is your guide to scoring phase V.

A: Even if you are not held accountable for problems the new ruling will cause, you still have to cope with them; in addition, you have done nothing to reopen communication with your professor. Further clashes are inevitable. Enter a score of zero on line 5 of your worksheet under 'personal' and/or 'group' score, if this was your choice, and/or that of the group.

B: You have reopened communication, but only to repeat your original position without attempt at negotiation. Your professor will probably feel she has no choice but to refuse you – and is probably still resentful about your attack on her. Another zero score.

C: Now you are showing understanding of the professor's position, and considering her needs as well as your own. It is to be hoped she is able to do likewise. Enter a score of ten points if you or the group made this choice.

D: You are facing the problem but delaying the confrontation. Postponing discussion will do nothing to resolve the problem – you need to achieve a new understanding with this woman. And you may find your own resentment growing as time passes unless you do something to dissipate it. However, since you do plan to get back to her, allow yourself (and/or your group) four points.

E: If you really did lose your temper, you should apologize – but at least you are implying regret. Also, you have reopened communication as soon as possible, and focused the problem. Allow yourself and your group seven points. When personal and group scores have been recorded correctly, turn to the next section.

Game phase VI: Defusing the conflict

Section 18

Assume that the professor is still angry as a result of your losing your temper with her, and that your first attempt to open communication did not calm her. When you go to her office now, she is still very hostile and speaks angrily to you. You realize it is time to end this quarrel, to lower the emotional climate, reduce the tension and begin to discuss the problem objectively. Here are some different ways of probing for the reasons behind hostile reactions:

- *Facts*: probe for the facts only.
- *Interpretation*: try to find reasons for the other's behaviour.
- *Judgment*: avoid being judgmental, that is, viewing the other person's behaviour as good or bad (or the person as a good person or a bad person).
- *Understanding*: demonstrate intellectual and emotional understanding of the other's point of view.
- *Support*: be supportive – express sympathy, fellow-feeling.

Without discussion, circle your personal choice to indicate which type of probe you think is illustrated in each of the statements in section 19. After you have circled your choices, compare them with those made by the other members of your team. Then select the statement that the group agrees would do most to lessen the conflict. Only a group choice is to be made. Enter the letter of this chosen statement on line 6 of the worksheet under 'group choice'. Then turn to section 20.

Section 19

Note: F = Facts
             I = Interpretation
             J = Judgment
             U = Understanding
             S = Support

Personal Choice					
F	I	J	U	S	**A.** I think you're reacting this way because you don't like it when somebody opposes your point of view.
F	I	J	U	S	**B.** Let's just sit down and talk about what's causing our problem.
F	I	J	U	S	**C.** I don't think you should lose your temper. In your position as associate professor in this school you really should be more careful how you react in a situation like this.
F	I	J	U	S	**D.** I understand that we've both become upset over this business. Can't we sit down together and talk about it?
F	I	J	U	S	**E.** I agree with your frustration over all this. I think there's something wrong if our system doesn't allow you a degree of flexibility in applying new rulings. Can we work our way out of this present problem?

Section 20: Results

This phase of the game does not call for a personal score. However, check your classifications with the following list:

A: interpretive

B: factual

C: judgmental

D: understanding

E: supportive

If your group chose B or D as the probe most likely to lessen conflict, enter ten points on line 6 of the worksheet under 'group choice'. One point is allowed for statements A and C, and three points for statement E.

The interpretive probe is argued to be more suitable when dealing with children; the judgmental probe is inflammatory; and the supportive probe, while concilatory, does not help to resolve the problem. In contrast, statements B and D (factual and understanding respectively) encourage problem-solving and open communication in an understanding atmosphere and would therefore probably do most to reduce the conflict.

When the group score has been entered, you are ready to turn to section 21.

Game phase VII: Creating an open communication climate

Section 21

To keep conflict to a minimum in an organization, communication must be free and open, since there are so many potential sources of conflict.

Without discussion, write a brief statement below, indicating what kind of relationship must exist if communication between peers is to be really open. After everybody has finished (after about seven minutes), turn to section 22, but not before.

Section 22: Results

Again without discussion, each participant reads their statement to the others. After everyone has had their turn, vote, by secret ballot on a blank piece of paper, for the best two sets of statements. (You may vote for your own.)

One member collects the ballots and announces the number of votes for each statement. Enter the votes your statement received on line 7a of the worksheet under 'votes' and, in addition, give yourself one vote for each of the thoughts below that was essentially covered by your notes on the previous section. Enter these additional votes on line 7b.

- A climate of trust must be established through honest dealings.
- Nothing that is said in the heat of discussion should be held later against the speaker.
- Nothing that is said should suggest that one person thinks they

know what the other is going to say or what they meant to imply.
- Wherever possible, what is said should be truthful but not so blunt as to hurt the other party. Opinion should be expressed impersonally.

Now see that all votes are correctly entered.

This is the end of the game. Add up your scores for phases I to VII and record them here.

Take some time to discuss your scores and your feelings about the game.

SNAKMAKERS

This is a game about marketing a product in a difficult sales environment. The players have to negotiate mutually opposing goals in a situation in which high mutual benefit is almost impossible. Information has to be managed in such a way that the parties are able to keep face in spite of threats to discredit them.

Time: at least half a day.
Number of players: about nine, minimum; preferably at least 12 to 15.
Materials:

- a description of the scenario and a rolecard for each player;
- writing materials (like order books) for the managers and representatives;
- cardboard and thick felt-tipped pens in various colours for the advertising people to make posters;
- enormous quantities of Smarties or M&Ms (chocolate buttons) and suitable containers to hold them;
- a sticky label for every player.

Scenario: SNAKMAKERS is a powerful multinational marketing company which has been criticized for an employment policy of discrimination against minorities and women. Among its many popular food products it sells a snack food in vast quantities – *Snaks*. However, there have been hints recently in the media that Snaks may contain carcinogenic ingredients. In other words, some people think eating Snaks may cause cancer – though there is no hard evidence for this.

To counter the adverse publicity, Snakmakers has decided to mount a public relations exercise and distribute free Snaks throughout the duration of the game – which represents any period of time, like a day, week or month. Each regional manager has been given a supply of Snaks to distribute through one or more sales representatives, working on commission, who will visit customers, offer them free samples and try to obtain written orders (secured by a cash deposit) for more Snaks at the standard retail price. Reps who secure these orders are entitled to half the deposit money, payable by the managers on return of each completed order form.

Snakmakers has also commissioned an advertising agency to promote Snaks because, since the adverse publicity, an active lobby has been directed against Snaks on health grounds.

Lobbyists will be visiting the customers to ask them to refuse the free samples and to sign a petition instead, calling for a ban on all Snaks, and to make a cash donation to pay for publicity. The lobbyists have set up a refreshment station in opposition to the Snaks team's gifts, offering free nutritious refreshments.

The job of the regional managers is to attract new customers for Snaks by organizing the distribution of free samples and the taking of orders. If there are many players, the managers can have assistants. The managers are in charge of at least one sales representative who does the actual legwork on commission, and they have access to the advice and assistance of the advertising agency (though if you only have a few players you may have to eliminate this). The managers are in charge of a supply of Snaks – which are real, like Smarties or M&Ms. They have to calculate how many Snaks they can afford to give away as free samples while leaving enough to fill urgent orders. Managers also have to work out the retail price, the deposit the reps must take from the customers with each order, and so on. They are also responsible for keeping a record of total customer orders, filling and supplying as many of them as they can during the course of the game.

The representatives know they are working on commission and that the object of the game as far as they are concerned is to earn as much money as possible by bribing customers with free samples to complete an order form and put down a deposit – of which they get to keep 50 per cent. The ad agents' job is to promote Snaks; while the anti-Snak lobbyists are passionately opposed to all

Snakmakers' products. The lobbyists are determined to undermine Snakmakers' sales and to lobby to have Snaks banned.

They try to persuade the ad agency to change sides and customers to refuse free samples of Snaks and give a donation to the cause instead. Customers are invited to visit the lobbyists' stall, take free and healthy refreshment and sign a petition.

The local member of parliament (or congressional representative), who is keeping an eye on the political implications of the campaign, assures the lobbyists that if there is sufficient public protest, s/he will back the lobby all the way – but meanwhile may decide to stay on good terms with the Snakmakers managers.

The customers represent the great retail buying public, spending their money to their own best advantage. At the start of the game they have all the power because they are the only players with any money (you can use real money or play money; we think real money adds spice to the game). Snakmakers and advertisers woo them with free samples and advertisements; lobbyists want their names on petitions. How they respond is up to them.

Roles and rules: to play SNAKMAKERS you need at least one large room without fixed furniture. The game is quite flexible. For example, you could play it in one of the public rooms of a hotel, as part of a conference, or in a theatre or rehearsal room. Arrange the room so that the three groups – Snakmakers, ad agents and lobbyists – each have an 'office' of table and chairs. Allocate the roles, give each player a copy of the game description as above, a rolecard and a sticky label to correspond with the role they are playing. Ask everybody to read carefully through the scenario and to start thinking about their individual roles. Ensure that they display their labels prominently (for example on their foreheads) because they have to know who everybody is. Explain that the only rules of the game are the constraints of the roles and the game setting. Within these limitations, the players should be allowed to take what action they wish to achieve their role objectives.

Allow everybody time to read the scenario and discuss the roles. After about ten minutes (or longer, if people ask for more time; but don't let them dawdle), ask the Snakmakers characters (managers and sales people), the advertising agents and the lobbyists to assemble at their respective tables – which you have clearly posted. The consumers remain where they are. Give group members time to become familiar with the contents of their tables. Meanwhile, divide all the money out between the consumers. Answer any questions, but briefly. You want to start the game as soon as you can after making sure that everybody knows what is happening and what they're supposed to do.

Announce that the game has begun. After this, take no further part in the action – observe and make notes but do not interfere (unless you feel you have to), even if requested to do so.

It is important to allow enough time for this game to develop, which is why we suggest you set aside half a day to play it. Coalitions will form, break up and reform if you let them and the results represent a fascinating microcosm of a free enterprise society.

Suggestions for discussion

It is quite feasible to use this game as a metaphor for industrial-relations disputes because the simulated environment of SNAKMAK-ERS is similar in many ways to real-life disputes between employers and unions for control of the workforce. Alternatively, you can debrief players in terms of the social responsibility owed by commercial enterprises to the wider society.

There is a battle ethos built into the game, as in IR or environmental confrontations. This atmosphere of 'winners and losers' and the pressures of commerce, added to people's normal reluctance to change their position, serve to reinforce – in the game and in real life – a wall of confrontation. In the face of this, individual players (Snakmakers or lobbyists) will probably have hesitated to suggest a modification of position, for fear of being thought a traitor to the cause. Moreover, teams tend to reinforce their internal optimism about 'winning' and can be very reluctant to examine the weaknesses in their positions. The first player to say something like: 'I don't think we should continue to sell this product; I think we will have to make a concession here' may well be subjected initially to attack by the rest of the team for letting the side down.

Another normal human characteristic is linked to a reluctance to change one's mind: the tendency to gloat over any retreat by one's opponent. Because SNAKMAKERS emphasizes the competitive elements in negotiation, the game is almost always played compet-itively. The lobbyists in particular are likely to claim 'victory' on the slightest grounds (as do trade-union representatives in real life); but in neither case can this be put down solely to bloody-mindedness. Lobbyists, like trade unionists, are accountable to their supporters in ways that employers are not, and therefore it is important to them that their activities are highly visible and seen as successful.

There are several lessons here for management: it pays, firstly, to have a thick skin over which insults pass harmlessly; and, secondly, to avoid becoming insulting. A more compliant attitude will make it easier for the other side to make concessions and move towards a situation of greater mutual benefit.

It often happens in SNAKMAKERS that the lobbyists and sales people quickly develop mutual hostility; but if one party, or even one individual, supplants this behaviour with a more conciliatory style, they are more likely to win over the other side. For example, one of the lobbyists once described in detail to the salespeople the death of her father (so she said) from cancer. The two saleswomen became deeply sympathetic and joined the ranks of the lobbyists.

SAFALA CAFE

This game illustrates the high mutual benefits a team can accrue when leadership is shared constructively between members. SAFALA CAFE also demonstrates that when one or more team members behave unconstructively, they have a dysfunctional effect on problem-solving and decision-making. In the game, each team member takes a specific negotiator role to solve a problem of concern to the whole group.

Time required: about two hours.
Number of players: from seven people upwards.
Materials: you will need to prepare a set of three envelopes according to the instructions below and enclose them in one large envelope.
Roles: seat each group of seven people round a table. Ask any observers to take notes when the negotiation begins. Tell everybody that group members will be asked to share leadership by taking particular roles. They will find out later how these roles are allocated. Meanwhile, you will describe the roles. Then give them the following written summary (one copy each) and go

through it with them till you're sure they understand the behaviour required for each role.

Summary of roles:

- *Information seeker.* This person's role will be to explore the dimensions of the problem as widely as possible on behalf of the team by asking questions and seeking to elicit all relevant information.
- *Compromiser/harmonizer.* This person will help maintain a relaxed and pleasant ambience within the group, an atmosphere in which problems can be discussed objectively and compromises found.
- *Clarifier.* This person will try to re-phrase others' statements when necessary, keep track of the discussion, summarize where needed, focus the task and generally assist communication between members.
- *Initiator.* This person's role will be to stimulate discussion, to initiate new ideas and press for solutions.
- *Avoider.* This person will seek to dispose of the problem in the least troublesome way.
- *Follower.* This will be a supportive role – to give positive feedback to reasonable suggestions, to be willing to undertake any tasks that seem likely to ease the process of solving the problem.
- *Information-giver.* This is an assertive, even aggressive role. The person who assumes it will not hesitate to state definite opinions about what the group should do to solve the problem.

When you have explained these roles and provided everybody with the written summary as above, put the large envelope (prepared as below) on the table in front of each group. Give no further instructions (except to ask them to open the envelope).

Preparing the envelopes

Write the following on the outside of the large envelope:

Enclosed in this package you will find three envelopes which contain directions for the phases of SAFALA CAFE. Open the package.

Now open envelope 1. Subsequent instructions will tell you when to open the others.

Envelope 1 contains:

- a copy of the following scenario for each player;
- a copy of the following 'instructions' for each player;
- seven small envelopes, each marked 'Rolecard' and containing a rolecard (as described below).

Contents of envelope 1

1. Scenario: you are all members of a newly established educational institution in a beachside resort about 100 miles from the city. Your college runs residential management-training courses and other organizational and staff-development programmes.

It is quite late in the evening and you have just completed a weekend course for 30 senior executives who are in a position, if they take away a good impression of the college, to send many students to your courses. All has gone well, except that some participants complained during the weekend about the facilities of the college, particularly the quality of the food and service in the college dining room.

All participants are now back in their residential accommodation, having a shower and getting changed before being picked up by you in two buses to be driven to a celebration dinner at Safala Cafe. This is a charming restaurant, nationally famous for its food, wine and service, in a historic location about 45 minutes' drive from the college. You are relying heavily on this dinner party to create a favourable atmosphere and smooth away any remaining traces of client dissatisfaction with the weekend.

However, you have just been informed that one bus is out of service. Therefore, half the executives will have to wait for 45 minutes while the other bus makes its run and returns. The same problem will have to be faced at the end of the evening. The college principal is away and cannot be consulted, but you know she is already worried about the overheads of this course, which has turned out to be more expensive than anticipated.

You have about 15 minutes in which to decide what to do.

2. Instructions for playing SAFALA CAFE, **phase 1** (one copy per team member).

Time allowed: 15 minutes.

Task: as described in the scenario.

Special instructions: each member is to take one of the smaller envelopes (how you allocate these is up to you) and follow their role instructions. Nobody is to reveal their instructions. After 15 minutes go on to the next envelope.

3. Rolecards (the players allocate these to each other).

- *Information seeker:* can the bus be fixed?
- *Compromiser/harmonizer:* we can stay with the group till the bus returns and ply them with liquor from the drinks cupboard to keep them happy.
- *Clarifier:* can we get in touch with the principal by telephone? What other possibilities are open to us?
- *Initiator:* we will have to book all the available taxis in the town, and worry about the expense later.
- *Avoider:* it's not our problem. We have to explain the situation to the group and let them decide if they want to wait or be taken to a restaurant in town.
- *Follower:* I've got a big car; I can transport six people.
- *Information-giver:* it will be impossible to get a booking at any restaurant in town at such short notice on a Sunday night. Some of the students will just have to wait.

Contents of envelope 2

Envelope 2 contains multiple copies (one for each team member) of the following:

Instructions for playing SAFALA CAFE, **phase II.**

Time allowed: five minutes.

Task: choose a group leader. When you have chosen, go on to the next envelope.

Contents of envelope 3

Envelope 3 contains multiple copies of the following:

Instructions for playing SAFALA CAFE, **phase III.**

Time allowed: ten minutes (or more if you wish).
Task: discuss the process by which you tried to solve the problem in phase I.
Special instructions: the group leader will lead this discussion.

Notes for discussion

1. Was leadership shared constructively between team members? Help participants to explore the power relationships that developed during the simulation.
2. Did anybody's behaviour in role appear non-constructive or actively destructive to decision-making? If so, does everybody clearly understand why?
3. Everybody had a specific negotiator role to play. Were they able to maintain it? If so, why? If not, why not? What effects on the negotiation did these roles have? How high were the mutual benefits of these role behaviours? When all groups have worked through the three envelopes, you can initiate a general debriefing session so that everybody can compare notes and discuss what behaviours seemed to be of high mutual benefit within a group, and which were not; and why.

MRP* (manufacturing resources planning): an information management simulation

This is a game in which players have to negotiate information in a series of steps in order to understand and learn a particular procedure. Its inventor was a consultant with an international management consultancy when he created MRP as an introduction to computer software for the manufacturing industry. We have also found his game very useful as a negotiation exercise to demonstrate the process of information management.

MRP requires quite a lot of work by you and your assistants, but it provides a powerful learning experience of the manufacturing industry and its hazards, and introduces all the relevant key concepts comparatively painlessly. Its learning 'builds' as the game progresses – players find themselves engrossed in an operation

---

* MRP was designed by a friend of ours, Vincent Ferravanti, director of systems analysis for AUGAT manufacturing company of Mansfield, Massachusetts, who kindly agreed to let us describe it here.

that becomes more entertainingly complex as they go on. When they come to apply these lessons to real life they are likely to be surprised by how much they have learned, particularly about the transition from a planned to a free-enterprise economy.

MRP was trialed at the 1990 conference of the International Simulation and Games Association (ISAGA) at the University of New Hampshire. Twenty-seven countries were represented – including many participants from East Europe – and players from Russia, Poland, East Germany, the UK, the Netherlands, USA and Japan took part in the game. MRP's economic lessons were the most valuable, according to these participants.

Scenario: players in teams experience all the essential processes of manufacture. They have to make decisions about quantities of product to be manufactured based on purchasing, marketing and sales estimates. The game is played in four sessions, each of a varying number of rounds, beginning with simple concepts and increasing in complexity session by session. Feedback to players is built into the design to demonstrate the essential importance of each of these processes.

Time required: the game is played in a total of thirteen rounds in five sessions. Each round lasts half an hour, the game effectively taking a whole day to play and debrief.

Number of players: minimum ten, to any number. In addition, you will need at least one co-director, because between you you have to play the supplier (wholesaler), purchaser (consumer) and banker, as well as being consultants once play begins.

Your consultancy role is necessary because players won't always grasp easily what they are expected to do: you and your colleagues will need to move helpfully from group to group during each round. You also need to make sure that players don't deviate from their instructions, at any rate during the first two or three rounds. Otherwise enterprising suppliers may immediately begin manufacturing and selling products at cut price to the consumers, who then default on their contracts with the 'factory', which as a result may go broke as early as round 3, which is disappointing for the players. While such market manipulations are OK in later rounds, you don't want the game to freewheel until you've established the basic manufacturing lessons of the earlier rounds, which are fundamentally what the game was designed to demonstrate.

Materials:

- A model car (or a model of any other 'product' which the players are going to manufacture) made of Lego blocks or any other 'raw materials'.

- Multiples of each part of the model. Quantities will depend on number of players and your estimate of how many models they can manufacture during the various rounds of the game. Your purchase of these game materials is likely to be quite a heavy capital item; however, you can use the parts over and over – not just for this game but for others in this book. There are many small construction kits available at toy shops nowadays – all they need to contain for your purposes are building materials and a blueprint for the finished product. If you are clever with your hands you can create your own. In any case you will have to make a model yourself which will go on display and to which the players will work.

- Writing materials for each playing group, and for your assistants/observers.

- One copy per player of written instructions for each round of the game, as indicated below.

- Large amounts of play money. We nearly got into trouble on one occasion by xeroxing US dollar bills in vast quantities. Hence we recommend you design your own artistic range – about £10,000 worth – of £10, £20, £50 and £100 notes, or any other currency. You will find this money very useful for other games as well.

Before the game

Get together with your colleague(s). Go through all instructions and materials. Work out prices of components and forecasts. For example, assume the model is made from the following Lego parts: 7 × A-bricks @ £10.00 each = £70.00; 1 × B-bricks @ £20.00 = £20.00; 1 × C-bricks @ £30.00 = £30.00; 1 × D-bricks @ £40.00 = £40.00. Total = £160.00. The price of the finished car to the consumer is £200.00.

This means each manufacturer will have to pay the suppliers a total of £160.00 to make each car and sell it to order for £200.00. If you forecast the number of car orders at ten that, say, factory 1 can handle, then this group should be issued with about £2000 in round 1. Theoretically, they should make a total profit overall of £400 – ie enough to make two more cars. Vary the forecasts from factory to factory, estimating smaller orders for the smaller groups and giving them comparatively less capital float. Make your forecasts on guesswork based on how long it took you to make the prototype.

Session I: Bill of materials (two rounds of half an hour)

At the start of the game, but before the first round: set yourselves up behind two large tables, on one of which the model and the supplies of its parts (each one priced) are displayed. The other table is for receipt and payment of forecast orders.

Divide the players into irregular-sized groups, with a minimum of three people in the smallest group. Introduce yourselves as wholesaler, consumer and (later in the game) banker.

When players are sitting in their groups, each at a table with their own construction space, give every person a copy of the following information, and clarify verbally any confusions.

Background information for players
Each group represents a manufacturing company. A model is on display of the product you are all going to manufacture, but if your company can design a more profitable model from the same parts you are welcome to do so. The model will remain on display so you can inspect it as closely and frequently as you wish.

Each company will need to purchase raw materials from the wholesaler and will be able to sell the finished products to the consumer.

Each group will give itself a name and organize itself into the following departments:

- purchasing (to be responsible for purchasing estimates);
- manufacturing (to be responsible for making the products according to the model);
- sales and marketing (to be responsible for sales forecasts and marketing the completed models).

The game will be played in five sessions over a total of 13 rounds, each of half an hour, and all business must be transacted within these rounds.

Give players plenty of time to absorb this information, to inspect the model and materials, and ask any questions. Meanwhile allocate the forecast money to each factory 'workbench'; then begin session 1, round 1.

Round 1

1. Announce that this session is called 'Bill of materials' and will be played in two rounds, each of half an hour. No business can be transacted between rounds.

2. Issue each group with one copy per person of a handout summarizing the following information:

- a description and price list of the parts required to make the cars (or whatever the product is);
- a sales forecast for round 2 (which is when the manufactured items will be sold);
- the current market price for the finished product - ie what the consumer will have to pay for it.

Each group has to decide how much it must buy of raw materials to fill its forecast orders. They must order this quantity from the wholesaler who will deliver the orders, after payment, immediately before the end of the round. That is, they cannot be used in manufacture till the beginning of the next round.

3. Now let players begin placing their orders for raw materials. If you feel able to cope with more variables here, you can arrange deliberately for supplies of parts to run low, then raise the price of the last of the stock and encourage purchasers to haggle over it.

Don't let anybody take any raw materials away. They have to be ordered and paid for. You deliver them just before the end of the round so that players can begin manufacture at the beginning of round 2.

Round 2

1. Explain that completed products must be kept in stock till the end of the round. They cannot be sold to the consumer one at a time.

2. Each group has now received its inventory (purchased supplies) and begins assembling the cars, or whatever the product is.

3. Make sure that representatives from each group are negotiating with you or your colleague as the wholesaler, to buy more parts to

be delivered at the end of the round as happened during round 1. You can give credit, if you want to add yet another dimension to the game (at a fairly high rate of interest).

4. Don't let the manufacturers sell their products item by item. They have to stockpile till they have completed their forecast orders. After 15 or 20 minutes, by which time all groups should have stockpiled a number of orders, indicate you and/or your colleague are now ready to start buying all the forecast orders. At this point you may find some groups have manufactured in excess of forecast orders while others may not have completed theirs.

5. Now collect the attention of everybody in the room (which may be difficult; you may need to blow a whistle). When you have comparative silence, announce a general trade recession. This means you will not be able to buy all the forecast orders. The result of this announcement will be that at least some forecasts have now turned out to be innacurate and some groups will be left with surplus stock.

6. You are now almost at the end of this round. Distribute any raw materials which have been ordered and paid for during the round.

By this time, some teams - if not all - should be in a state of confusion; for example, some may have too little money, or too many manufactured items that they can't sell because of the restricted market.

Now call a break, say of half an hour, to allow people rest and refreshment and the chance to discuss with you and with each other what has happened in the game so far. You will probably need this break too, to catch up with events, to estimate the manufacturing capacity of each team, and so that you can give a summary of the action to the whole group when it reassembles. When everybody seems clear about what happened and why, start Session II.

Session II: Capacity (played over two rounds)

Round 1 (half an hour)
1. At the start of this round, give each group a fixed capacity for their manufacture in any one round (you should by this time have a fair idea of the manufacturing capacity of each group). Explain that any group can exceed its given capacity by paying you and/or

your colleague – in your role as the wholesaler – a 'shift differential'. Make this an arbitary sum, say £100.

2. Now give each group a new forecast. Make sure that the forecast for every team exceeds the fixed capacity you have just assigned to it.

3. Groups now begin assembling their products and stockpiling them as before for sale at the end of the round. Meanwhile, they buy more supplies to be delivered at the end of the round (you can recycle raw materials by cannibalizing the cars purchased at the end of the first session). Manufacturers also negotiate shift differentials if they want these.

4. After about 20 minutes, indicate that products may now be sold and new supplies delivered. Then signal the end of the round.

Round 2 (half an hour)

This round proceeds as in 3 and 4 above. At the end of the round ask each group to make an inventory of parts purchased, goods sold and cash in hand. Announce as winner the company with the most money. Discuss the reasons for your decision.

Session III: Forecasting demands (in two rounds)

Round 1 (half an hour)

1. Before signalling the beginning of round 1, distribute a handout with the following information for each player:

Handout:

The forecast is now a total market forecast, instead of each company being given its individual forecast.

In other words, the forecast is that (say) *30 products in all* will be purchased at the end of the round.

There is nothing to indicate which company or companies will be asked to supply these 30 manufactured items (cars or whatever).

Though previously all such goods have been purchased at a fixed price, now the individual manufacturers may ask any price they choose and the consumer is free to buy as many or as few as s/he wishes from each group, so long as the total comes close to the total market forecast.

---

2. Now signal that round 1 has begun. It is played on the same lines as all the other rounds.

Round 2 (half an hour)

By this time all groups should be engaged in purchasing – deciding what to buy and when – and manufacturing their products while deciding on market capacity and projected sales figures. These estimates will be calculated on the going price of the product.

At the end of round 2, ask for another inventory from each group and find out which company has the most money. Initiate a general discussion as to why.

Session IV: Order policy and scrap factors (in four rounds, each of half an hour)

1. Before beginning the first round, distribute another handout with this information:

Handout:

Each raw material part now has a minimum and a maximum order quantity. For example, if players are working with Lego bricks, then perhaps A-bricks must be bought in lots of 70 and any one order may not exceed 100 bricks.

Each part also has a scrap factor. In the Lego example, for every 14 A-bricks, you might instruct that one has to be discarded.

---

2. Now start round 1 and continue through rounds 2, 3 and 4 as for previous sessions. At the end of round 4, take another inventory and find the company with the most money.
3. On the basis of their performance during this session, each group is now given a market forecast. By this time you should be able to estimate this fairly easily.

Session V: The cost of holding inventory (three rounds, each of half an hour)

1. Before the first round begins, collect all inventories, and all the money from all groups.
2. Now introduce a bank which can lend money at a fixed rate of interest per round. The bank will also pay interest on deposits at a

fixed rate, slightly less than the lending rate. The bank can lend money up to a fixed amount. This amount will be calculated on the borrowing group's assets.

3. Give a total market sales forecast, based on previous total sales figures.

4. Announce (after a blast on the whistle to attract attention), or circulate a written announcement, that the price of the Lego bricks (or whatever the raw materials are) will vary from now on, depending on supply and demand.

5. Announce that as the consumer you will now modify actual purchases in terms of the sales forecast. In other words, you may decide your purchases will exceed or fall short of the forecast.

6. Three rounds are now played as before, after which the overall winners are announced. The winning group will have the most money after settling up with the bank.

This is the final round of MRP, and players will have participated in it for most of the day, allowing for meals and coffee breaks. If you have introduced the game as part of a residential course, conference, or some similar activity over several days, you may want to leave a final debriefing till the day following the game.

* * *

MRP is the last game in this book. We have saved it till now because it is both the most highly structured and most complex of all the games. It is also one of the most rewarding for two reasons: after playing it, participants should be able to identify the problems of manufacturing resources planning, describe its processes and follow its procedures; players should be able to differentiate between the tasks of MRP in a non-competitive and a competitive environment.

Finally, MRP is rich in a sense that all the preceding games share: after participating in them, players should be able to discuss implications for real life that had not previously occurred to them. Assessment of learning outcomes from simulations and games is always difficult, which is why simulations like MRP are of special interest; they are comparatively easy to evaluate, having specific and measurable learning objectives.

We have tried to strike a balance in this book between games like MRP that can be subjected to empirical assessment, and more experiential exercises (like ROSEMARY'S RIVER, for example) that rely for evaluation almost entirely on the players' anecdotal evidence. We hope that every time you play games with students you will use some kind of evaluation instrument afterwards, even as basic as the example we include in Appendix 2 at the end of the book. Every piece of evidence is valuable in the continuous effort by gamers to establish the learning that participants derive from games, roleplays, improvisations and simulations – learning that they could not have acquired without 'playing the game'.

Alphabetical List of Games According to Topic

Virtually all the activities described in this book cover the whole range of negotiation skills. The only way it has been possible to compile the following list is to indicate the major emphasis of each exercise.

Topic	Title	Activity	Page
Adversary relations	OTTO'S GAME	game	51
	WIN-LOSE	game	64
Alternative strategies	GETTING THERE	game	38
Attitudes, emotions,	DAVID'S DILEMMA	game	56
beliefs and perceptions	FOUR LETTER WORDS	game	48
	ROSEMARY'S RIVER	game	54
Bargaining, compromise and concession-making	MONUMENTAL	simulation	122
Collaborative adversaries: costs and benefits in negotiation	COLLABORATIVE ADVERSARY	game	66
	TOWN AND GOWN	improvisation	107
Compromise and conflict resolution	BUSINESS SCHOOL	simulation	130
Crosscultural communication	APPLIED METALS	roleplay	74
	CORPORAL PUNISHMENT	roleplay	81
	DOG'S DINNER	roleplay	82
	FORCED CHOICE	roleplay	77
	FOREIGN BODY	roleplay	75
	HOMEWORK	roleplay	82
	LATE ARRIVAL	roleplay	78
	SUPERMARKET	improvisation	79
Ethics and social responsibility: mutually opposing goals	SNAKMAKERS	simulation	149
	LALAIKA	game	61
Feedback	LISTENING	game	57

Topic	*Title*	*Activity*	*Page*
Hidden agendas and positional bargaining	YO SOY BEAN	simulation	116
Industrial relations and collective bargaining: pre-negotiation strategies and 'bottom lines' in negotiation	THE RBO GAME RELOCATION SILVERWOOD	improvisation improvisation game	99 96 67
Information management	MRP	simulation	157
Joint problem-solving, leadership and teamwork	CHAIN OF COMMAND SAFALA CAFE	game simulation	42 153
Making excuses, saying no gracefully; saving face and prevaricating	NO MAYBE	game	40
Negotiating style: avoiding false positions	PLAYBACK	improvisation	86
Negotiating written meanings	GOING FINISH	improvisation	91
Objectivity: seeing others' viewpoints	DEVIL'S ADVOCATE	improvisation	83
Planning	BLUEPRINT	game	58
Violence (negotiating violence)	MERI WANTAIM MAN	game	70

Alphabetical List of Games

APPLIED METALS
Type of activity: roleplay; semi-structured duologue.
Objectives: to practise interpersonal communication, conflict resolution and persuasion in cross-cultural settings.
Time required: about an hour if several pairs of students take it in turns to enact the roleplay, followed by general class discussion.
Number of players: any number

BLUEPRINT
Type of activity: team game in which members compete to make a model.
Objectives: to illustrate differences in task perception between short- and long-term planners.
Time required: about an hour.
Number of players: virtually any number, in small groups.

BUSINESS SCHOOL
Type of activity: simulation game for players to work through on their own.
Objectives: to enable players to work as individuals and as team members to solve interpersonal conflict in a work environment.
Time required: about two hours.
Number of players: any number can play, in work groups.

CHAIN OF COMMAND
Type of activity: team game.
Objectives: to illustrate the need for joint problem-solving as well as leadership in work groups. Members have to pool individual pieces of information to understand the task.
Time required: about an hour.
Number of players: any number from about five.

COLLABORATIVE ADVERSARY

Type of activity: a building game.

Objectives: to demonstrate the advantages of collaboration over conflict between groups, if all group members are to achieve their various needs.

Time required: about half an hour.

Number of players: any number.

CORPORAL PUNISHMENT

Type of activity: drama improvisation on the theme of corporal punishment in schools.

Objectives: to illustrate cross-cultural differences in social norms.

Time required: about an hour to set up and enact, and about another hour for discussion afterwards.

Number of players: any number from about five.

DAVID'S DILEMMA

Type of activity: narrative, followed by class discussion.

Objectives: to demonstrate how people's value-judgments colour their perceptions of a situation and their attitudes towards the behaviour of the people in it.

Time required: about half an hour.

Number of players: any number.

DEVIL'S ADVOCATE

Type of activity: debate. Players have to adopt first one point of view on a given issue and argue it, then argue the opposite viewpoint.

Objectives: to provide players with practice in objective argument and to demonstrate the advantages of being able to see more than one viewpoint rather than having a fixed bottom line in negotiation.

Time required: about an hour.

Number of players: any number over three.

DOG'S DINNER

Type of activity: drama improvisation on the theme of other people's eating/cooking habits.

Objectives: to illustrate cross-cultural differences in social norms.

Time required: about an hour.

Number of players: any number.

FORCED CHOICE

Type of activity: roleplay; a semi-structured duologue.
Objectives: to give students in cross-cultural contexts the opportunity to practise interpersonal negotiation skills.
Time required: about an hour if several pairs of students in turn enact the roles, followed by general class discussion.
Number of players: any number over two.

FOREIGN BODY

Type of activity: roleplay; semi-structured duologue.
Objectives: to give students in cross-cultural contexts the opportunity to practise interpersonal negotiation skills.
Time required: about an hour if several pairs of students in turn enact the roleplay, followed by general class discussion.
Number of players: any number over two.

FOUR LETTER WORDS

Type of activity: a game about attitudes towards negotiation: players have to agree on the nature of the task before trying to complete it.
Objectives: to illustrate how perception of a task will fundamentally affect the nature of problem-solvers' solutions.
Time required: about an hour.
Number of players: any number over five.

GETTING THERE

Type of activity: competitive team game.
Objectives: to demonstrate adversary relationships and behaviour and their results.
Time required: about half an hour.
Number of players: enough to form two teams, say ten players in all, minimum, with virtually no maximum.

GOING FINISH

Type of activity: bargaining game between pairs of players.
Objectives: to apply basic criteria to assess the value of written information in terms of the reader's needs.
Time required: at least an hour, preferably longer.
Number of players: at least two, preferably at least three to five players.

HOMEWORK

Type of activity: cross-cultural roleplay, structured dialogue.

Objectives: to illustrate how misunderstandings can arise from imperfect knowledge of the other's phraseology, use of language, etc. Designed to illustrate cross-cultural differences in perception of what is and what is not 'bad language'.

Time required: about an hour to set up, enact and debrief.

Number of players: any number from about five.

LALAIKA

Type of activity: task-oriented competitive team game.

Objectives: to illustrate the ethics of industrial relations and the social responsibility of organizations to the wider environment.

Time required: about two hours.

Number of players: any number from about five.

LATE ARRIVAL

Type of activity: roleplay; semi-structured duologue.

Objectives: to practise cross-cultural interpersonal resolution of conflict/misunderstanding.

Time required: about an hour if several pairs of students in turn enact the roleplay, followed by general class discussion.

Number of players: any number over two.

LISTENING

Type of activity: game.

Objectives: to demonstrate the need to get feedback from receivers to ensure senders' messages have been understood as encoded.

Time required: about half an hour.

Number of players: any number.

MERI WANTAIM MAN

Type of activity: board game with floor cloth of squares on which players become the pieces in a game like Snakes and Ladders, moving up or down the board depending on message cards drawn from a pack.

Objectives: to identify more or less effective strategies to handle domestic violence; can be adapted to other topics.

Time required: about two hours.

Number of players: three to seven: any more, and another 'board' would be required.

MONUMENTAL

Type of activity: simulation game between collaborative adversaries.

Objectives: to identify the most effective strategies for bargaining between people who need to collaborate in a business enterprise but whose individual interests are mutually opposed.

Time required: Can be played in about two hours, or can be expanded to take most of the day, or even to run over several days.

Number of players: at least five; up to any number.

MRP

Type of activity: simulation game which ideally requires at least two game directors.

Objectives: the title is short for 'materials resources planning' and the game was designed to introduce players, round by round, to the complexities of this activity in the manufacturing industry. It is also an illustration of the transition from a planned economy to a free-enterprise society.

Time required: at least a day.

Number of players: six to 15; any more, and the game is difficult to manage without a team of game directors.

NO MAYBE

Type of activity: quiz game.

Objectives: to identify a number of effective tactics and manoeuvres for avoiding a direct 'yes' or 'no' in bargaining while keeping negotiation open. The game also provides insights to Japanese negotiation styles.

Time required: about an hour.

Number of players: three to seven.

OTTO'S GAME

Type of activity: syndicate gambling game using packs of cards.

Objectives: to demonstrate how and why coalitions are formed and broken; to identify cultural differences in the way societies treat their less productive members.

Time required: about an hour.

Number of players: virtually any number from about seven.

PLAYBACK

Type of activity: group improvisation. Players have to devise a public relations/publicity campaign.

Objectives: to help players identify their own negotiation styles, and recognize how to apply these styles appropriately in negotiation to achieve their objectives.

Time required: two to four hours, depending on number of players.

Number of players: five to 15 players.

RBO

Type of activity: industrial relations improvisation.

Objectives: the name stands for 'relationship by objectives' and it was designed to illustrate McGregor's 'Theory Y' principle of workplace motivation.

Time required: a day.

Number of players: virtually any number from about seven.

RELOCATION

Type of activity: industrial relations improvisation between two teams of players.

Objectives: to identify and find ways to overcome conflicts of interests and non-productive behaviour in negotiation between employers, employees and worker representatives.

Time required: about an hour and a half.

Number of players: minimum six, to virtually any number.

ROSEMARY'S RIVER

Type of activity: narrative followed by class discussion.

Objectives: to identify ways in which people's value judgments will colour their perceptions of a situation and affect their attitudes towards the behaviour of the people in it.

Time required: about half an hour.

Number of participants: any number.

SAFALA CAFE

Type of activity: simulation in which individuals have jointly to solve a transportation crisis. Players have specific roles to play, hence the need to resolve individual differences of opinion before the problem can be solved.

Objectives: to identify real-life 'strategic roles' people tend to adopt in negotiation; and to describe tactics to combine these roles into effective problem-solving.
Time required: about one and a half hours.
Number of players: about five in each group.

SILVERWOOD
Type of activity: improvisation. Players work on an improvised group project in their spare time.
Objectives: to identify the concepts of industrial democracy in work relationships.
Time required: this activity was designed to run over days or even weeks as a group exercise in players' own time during a seminar or course.
Number of players: virtually any number over four or five.

SNAKMAKERS
Type of activity: simulation game. Sales teams have to overcome marketplace resistance and active lobbying against their product on health and safety grounds.
Objectives: to identify strategies for overcoming organized resistance; to discuss business ethics and social responsibility; to practise persuasion.
Time required: at least two hours, or can be expanded to take most of the day, or even to run over several days, depending on numbers of players.
Number of players: about nine, preferably 12 to 15.

SUPERMARKET
Type of activity: group roleplay/improvisation on the theme of 'jumping the queue' in a supermarket.
Objectives: to identify some of the major ways in which cross-cultural misunderstandings and conflicts can arise.
Time required: at least an hour.
Number of players: five to 15.

TOWN AND GOWN
Type of activity: improvisation about collaborative adversaries.
Objectives: to illustrate the importance and high mutual benefits of resolving conflict among various groups with different priorities

but similar overall goals; to identify strategies, tactics and manoeuvres for achieving these high mutual benefits.

Time required: the game can last from about two hours to virtually the whole day, depending on numbers and the needs of the group.

Number of players: minimum of ten.

WIN-LOSE

Type of activity: game.

Objectives: to identify and demonstrate manipulative/persuasive tactics to achieve hidden agendas; the effects of this behaviour on those it is directed against.

Time required: about half an hour.

Number of players: five upwards.

YO SOY BEAN

Type of activity: cross-cultural simulation game. Sellers and buyers have to negotiate the sale/purchase of a food consignment under language difficulties and conditions of mutual distrust.

Objectives: to identify the dysfunctional and other results of mutual suspicion and distrust on bargaining outcomes.

Time required: can be played in about two hours or can be expanded to take most of the day, or even to run over several days.

Number of players: two teams of three to five.

Appendix 1: Definitions and Principles in Negotiating Industrial Disputes – Causes and Tactics

Precedent arguments

These are arguments using past events as justification for present/future claims/situations: what has happened before has been accepted and the circumstances here are similar.

Merit arguments

Such arguments are used when there is no clear past guide (for example because a new set of circumstances has arisen). It is important to recognize that merit arguments are based upon what a society regards as 'just'. Clearly, such definitions vary between societies and over time, and often become enshrined in law. It is therefore difficult to summarize merit arguments. However, the following guidelines may help.

Natural justice

The principle of a fair hearing of both sides before a decision is made – the principle of impartiality. Bias should not be allowed to affect the result.

Fairness

Being fair usually means that everybody should be treated the same; that workers should be entitled to expect a fair reward for fair work; that people should be given a choice.

Reasonableness

Being reasonable includes the culture-specific concepts that people should not be treated harshly, placed in unnecessary danger or asked to behave in a dishonest, immoral or unconscionable manner. Moreover people should be given adequate time, training and notice when confronted with change, and so on.

These principles should be seen in the context of the distribution of power in any given situation. The perception of power is an inherent part of negotiating. It can be the impetus for agreement being finalized or in obtaining the initial commitment to negotiate. The perception and distribution of power can therefore be critical in determining the outcome of a negotiation and the way in which that outcome is reached.

Although many general reasons have been given for the existence of industrial disputes, most practitioners are confronted by the immediate causes or reasons, usually stated in the form of claims or demands. These are the main ones:

- wages, salaries and allowances;
- working conditions;
- safety and health;
- hours of work;
- leave;
- discipline;
- dismissal;
- redundancy;
- changed work practices;
- demarcation (which employees from which trade union should perform which tasks);
- jurisdictional (also between trade unions, over which union covers which group or groups of workers);
- union membership;
- award interpretation;
- political and social issues;
- managerial prerogatives.

Tactics employed by trade unions:

- strikes;
- bans and limitations.

Tactics employed by employers:

- transfer of troublesome employees to situations where they can do less harm;
- shift production: move the factory or office to another part of the country or overseas;
- sub-contract: get the work done outside the organization;
- discipline of individuals or groups of workers;
- lay-offs;
- dismissal.

Appendix 2: Evaluation Form

The following is an example of an evaluation form that game directors might ask players to complete after a roleplay, improvisation, game or simulation.

Evaluation

Please give a score out of 10 to each of the qualities below (where 10 is the best standard you can imagine, 0 is the worst and 5 is barely adequate).

Quality	*Score*
Relevance of subject matter	. . . .
The way things were organized	. . . .
Level of interest maintained	. . . .
Competence of the presenter	. . . .
Your own performance	. . . .

Now, in a few words, say what you think about the activity, and this type of experience-based training. For example:

- its most useful/least useful aspects;
- anything important left out;
- how it could be improved.

General Bibliography

Berne, Eric (1984) *Games People Play* Harmondsworth: Penguin.

Casse, Pierre and Deol, Surinder (1985) *Managing Intercultural Negotiations* Washington DC: SIETAR International.

Christopher, Elizabeth M and Smith, Larry E (1987) *Leadership Training Through Gaming: Power, People and Problem-solving* London: Kogan Page. (*Note: Negotiation Training Through Gaming* is in a sense a 'follow-up' to this earlier book. It describes a variety of games, roleplays, simulations and other activities concerning leadership. The authors draw heavily on situational leadership theorists such as Fiedler, Hersey and Blanchard, Blake and Mouton. The book is divided into several sections, including one on games for young players. This section represents the experiences of one of the authors, who was for a time youth leadership training officer for a group of young people with behavioural and social problems. The book also benefits from both authors' experience of gaming in cross-cultural and multinational contexts.)

Christopher, Elizabeth M and Smith, Larry E (1990) Shaping the content of simulation/games, in Crookall, David and Oxford, Rebecca L (eds) *Simulation Gaming and Language Learning* New York: Newbury House. (*Note:* This book chapter argues that because simulation/games are models of social organization in the 'real' world, teachers' fundamental beliefs about the nature of social organization - their 'worldview' - will affect the structure and organization of any simulation/game they design and/or present. It is further argued that the content of any dynamic structure is in continual interaction with the form in which it is arranged and presented: therefore the content of all simulation games - irrespective of their subject-matter - will inevitably reflect the worldview of their creators whether they are consciously aware of it or not.

The chapter suggests that there are basically two models of game structure, each representing a different and opposing value system. The chapter identifies the salient characteristics of each model, suggests how these will affect the responses of the game participants, and offers guidelines for game presenters to enhance or subvert either model at will, depending on their teaching needs.)

Deutsch, M (1973) *The Resolution of Conflict; Constructive and Destructive Processes* New Haven CT: Yale UP.

Donahue, William A, Diez, Mary E and Hamilton, Mark (1984) Coding naturalistic negotiation interaction, *Human Communication Research* 10, 3, spring 1984, 403–25.

Drucker, P F (1954) *The Practice of Management* New York: Harper and Row.

Fisher, Glen (1980) *International Negotiation: A Cross-cultural Perspective* Chicago: Intercultural Press Inc.

Fisher, Roger and Ury, William (1988) *Getting to Yes* Harmondsworth: Penguin.

Fowler, Alan (1986) *Effective Negotiation* London: British Institute of Personnel Management.

Graham, John L and Sano, Yoshihiro (1984) *Smart Bargaining: Doing Business with the Japanese* Cambridge Mass: Ballinger Publishing Company. (*Note*: This book represents a genuine attempt by the authors to bridge communication gaps between American negotiators and their Japanese counterparts. It is perhaps inevitable that non-American readers will find it somewhat ethnocentric. The authors argue that because negotiation is by definition a situation of interdependence, Americans are not well equipped, historically, traditionally and culturally, to handle it. They identify a 'John Wayne' syndrome in which the 'typical or dominant behavior of American negotiators' is confrontational, independent, informal, impatient and argumentative. They contrast this with the Japanese negotiation style which they describe as dependent, formal, long-term oriented, patient and oblique. The book is included in this bibliography because one of our games (NO MAYBE) is based on the table on p 24, 'Sixteen ways the Japanese avoid saying no'.)

Jandt, Fred Edmund and Gillette, Paul (1985) *Win–Win Negotiating: Turning Conflict into Agreement* New York: John Wiley & Sons. (*Note*: This book is an expansion and elaboration of a professional development seminar, 'Managing conflict productively', which explained how conflict in organizations can be controlled and used and how managers can become more adept as negotiators within and without their organizations. There are many real-life examples to illustrate the arguments.

The authors explain why conflict is inevitable within organizations, and how small conflicts can quickly become large ones. They discuss the productive as well as destructive effects of conflict, describe how to identify sources of conflict and offer practical suggestions on how to avoid it or deal with it.)

Kennedy, G, Benson, J and MacMillan, J (1980) *Managing Negotiations* London: Business Books.

Kolb, David, Rubin, Irwin and McIntyre, John (1986) *Organizational Psychology: A Book of Readings* New Jersey: Prentice Hall.

McGrath, J E (1966) A social psychological approach to the study of negotiation, in Bowers, R (ed) *Studies on Behaviour in Organizations; A Research Symposium* Athens, Georgia: University of Georgia Press, pp 101–34.

McGregor, Douglas (1960) *The Human Side of Enterprise* New York: McGraw-Hill.

March, Robert M (1988) *The Japanese Negotiator: Subtlety and Strategy Beyond Western Logic* Tokyo: Kodansha International.

Mintzberg, H (1973) *The Nature of Managerial Work* New York: Harper and Row.

Morley, Ian and Stephenson, Geoffrey (1977) *The Social Psychology of Bargaining* London: George Allen and Unwin.

Myers, M Scott (1978) *Managing with Unions* Reading, Mass: Addison-Wesley.

Pruitt, Dean G and Carnevale, Peter J D (1982) *The Development of Integrative Agreements, Cooperation and Helping Behavior: Theories and Research* New York: Academic Press.

Putman, L I and Jones, T S (1982) Reciprocity in negotiations: an analysis of bargaining interaction, *Communication Monograph* 49, pp 71–191.

Sleigh, John (1989) *Making Learning Fun* Wollongong, New South Wales: John Sleigh Publications.

Tung, Rosalie L (1984) *Business Negotiations with the Japanese* Lexington, Mass: Lexington Books

Via, Richard and Smith, Larry E (1979) *Talk and Listen* Oxford: Pergamon.

Wall, James A Jr (1985) *Negotiation: Theory and Practice* Glenview Ill: Scott Foresman & Co.

Simulations and Games Bibliography

Armstrong, R H R and Taylor, John L (eds) (1970) *Instructional Simulation Systems in Higher Education* Cambridge Institute of Education. (Introduces the concept of simulation games and provides examples.)

—— (1971) *Feedback on Instructional Simulation Systems* Cambridge Institute of Education. (Feedback includes discussion of effectiveness of games and simulations, use of video in simulation games and comparisons between different game techniques.)

Boocock, S S and Schild, E O (eds) (1968) *Simulation Games in Learning* Sage. (The classic book of readings on simulation games.)

Clarke, M (1978) *Simulations in the Study of International Relations* Ormskirk: Hesketh.

Duke, R D (1974) *Gaming, the Future's Language* New York: Wiley.

Heitzman, William Ray (1983) *Educational Games and Simulations* Washington DC: National Education Association. (Slight, but a good summary of play theory and research findings on play techniques for learning.)

Jones, Ken (1980) *Simulations: A Handbook for Teachers* London: Kogan Page and New York: Nichols Publishing. (Discusses the meaning of simulation games and describes some classic game designs such as STARPOWER; also advises on choosing, using and assessing simulation games; includes a good bibliography.)

Jones, Ken (1988) *Interactive Learning Events: A Guide for Facilitators* London: Kogan Page.

Jones, Ken (1989) *A Sourcebook of Management Simulations* London: Kogan Page and New York: Nichols Publishing.

Jones, Ken (1990) *Icebreakers: A Sourcebook of Games, Exercises and Simulations* London: Kogan Page and San Diego: University Associates.

McGuire, Christine H, Solomon, Lawrence M and Bashook, Philip G (1976) *Construction and Use of Written Simulations* USA: The Psychological Corporation. (The game strategies described here are forerunners of computer-based training methods, for example: 'If you choose answer #1, turn to Section 0'; and so on.)

Maidment, Robert and Bronstein, Russell H (1973) *Simulation Games, Design and Implementation* Columbus Ohio: Chas Merrill.

Taylor, J L and R A Walford (1972) *Simulation in the Classroom* Milton Keynes: Open University Press. (An introduction to roleplay, games and simulations in education, with six established games described in detail and a directory of relevant published material.)

—— (1978) *Learning and the Simulation Game* Milton Keynes: Open University Press.

Thiagarajan, Sivasailam and Stolovitch, Harold D (1978) *Instructional Simulation Games* Englewood Cliffs NJ: The Instructional Design Library vol 12, Educational Technology Publications.

Index

187